ALL OF
BRITTANY

Texts by:
PATRICK ANDRÉ
Professor of History and Archaeology - Vannes

ROGER BARRIÉ
Regional curator of the Inventaire Général - Rennes

YVES-PASCAL CASTEL
Researcher of the Inventaire - Morlaix

ERIC COUTUREAU
Curator of the Inventaire Général - Nantes

RENÉ LE BIHAN
Curator of the Musée municipal of Brest

PHILIPPE PETOUT
Curator of the Musées de Saint-Malo

JEAN-JACQUES RIOULT
Curator of the Inventaire Général - Rennes

NICOLAS SIMONNET
Curator of Mont-Saint-Michel

BONECHI

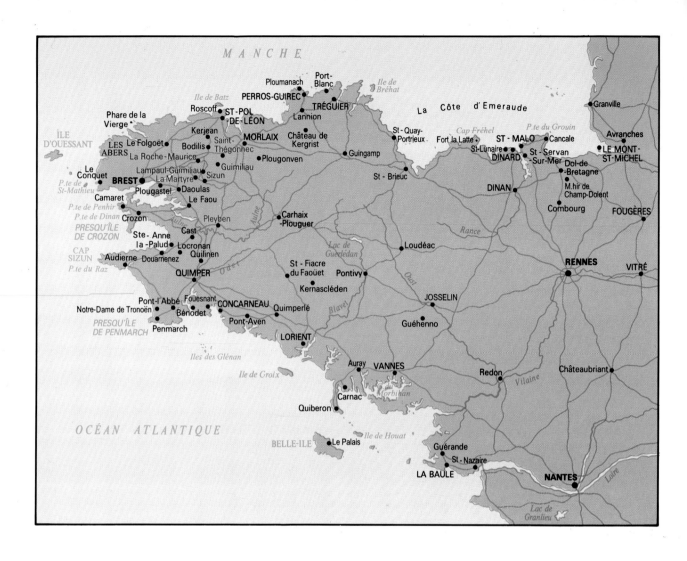

INTRODUCTION

The romantic image of which Brittany is prisoner may be justified but is much too limited and does not take due consideration of the topographical, historical and cultural reality, first and foremost the sea — the Atlantic Ocean and the English Channel which embrace the Armorican peninsula, the Armor, so vast a stretch of land that the inhabitants of the interior, the Argoat, forget the very presence of the sea. A land of seafarers, Brittany is also a land of country-people and their ancient rural dwellings are among the loveliest still to be found. The presence of the sea evokes a land of mists and fogs, with ever-changing skies — the reason why so many painters tried to capture the extraordinary quality of the light here on their canvases. This watery land, so often at the mercy of the storms, with its melancholy moors and its age-old mountain massif, can also be a friendly smiling country-side, peaceful and picturesque with its jagged coastline and verdant vales. Granite, in its different aspects, grey, blue or rose, is to be found everywhere, but it is accompanied by other materials long in use: grey, green blue and mauve slate; beige sandstone; conchiferous limestone or micaceous chalk of the Loire, pisé and wood and even marble imported from the Maine. The ancient and mysterious forests are no longer simply the refuge of King Arthur and Merlin. They have unstintingly provided the wood which the Breton coopers have so skillfully used since the Middle Ages. Then in the Ancien Régime it was a land to be exploited for its silver and iron mines. To the 17th-century Parisian, Brittany was synonymous with the last reaches of civilization. As a matter of fact, in the Middle Ages it was at the very heart of the Atlantic world, a mercantile center known from the Mediterranean to the Baltic, and the font which furnished products such as the canvas used to equip the ships of Charles V. This role continued with the opening up of the New World.

The fundamental strong organization of the parishes resulted in an awareness of their collective identity. Thanks to this and the rise of its princes it was a veritable Breton state that played a part in the international diplomacy between France and England until it was transformed into a wise province after the royal weddings of the duchess Anne in the 16th century. Indeed, ever since the Roman conquest, Brittany had been a land of aperture and welcome thanks to the sea, the Loire and its frontiers. When we think of Brittany today it is as a site favored by prehistoric civilizations who left their megalithic monuments, exceptional in the West, here. But in the 6th century the immigration of populations from across the English Channel overlaid the strongly Romanized Celtic-Gallic substrata with an authentic version of Christianity. Dolmens and menhirs stand side by side with the magnificent manifestations of a Christian culture that was both universal and specific, like the language in its Breton and Welsh versions.

It has often been remarked that archaism and cultural lag are characteristic of a rural civilization. The history of art in Brittany shows both the assimilation of various cultures and the chronological accumulation of innovations. In a process of cultural capitalization, the towns as well as the countryside rapidly accepted all modes of artistic expression, Gothic art as well as the Renaissance aesthetic, the geometric art of the Celts and the color and the formal aspects of the abstract art of the 20th century. With this wealth of experience and gifted with a capacity for evolution, Brittany remains, in its own personal way, the farthermost tip of Europe.

Place du Champ-Jacquet: the large gabled house to the right has been faithfully restored with its unbroken horizontal glazing. The one on the left, which is later, was plastered with an alternation of solid and void as in stone architecture.

Facing page, above: two twin canonical houses, at the apse of the cathedral. Even though they date to the early 16th century, the moulding of the crossbeams and the decoration of the wooden brackets is still very Gothic.

Rue du Chapitre, below, left, a large corner house of the last quarter of the 16th century. On the right, in the Rue Saint-Michel, the picturesque facades jostle each other.

RENNES

Until the fire of 1720 Rennes, a city of paradoxes, was built mostly of wood, breaking loose from the cliché which equivalates Brittany with granite. It was founded where the Ille and the Vilaine rivers flow together, as indicated in its Celtic name, *Condate*, which means confluent. These courses of water which were originally so essential were canalized in the 19th century and later partially covered over. At first sight nothing can be seen of the ancient city of *Riedones*, and yet it is all there under our feet. The cathedral, rebuilt more than once, still stands on the site of the first house of worship. The original settlement was enclosed by a wall built in haste at the time of the unrest in the 3rd century. During the 15th century the uneasy proximity of the French-English conflict led the dukes to reinforce the defenses of the town. The original wall was repaired and reinforced with towers; to the east a second wall enclosed the Ville-Neuve of the merchants; lastly on the south, on the other side of the Vilaine, a third wall safeguarded the district of the textile and leather workers, whose numbers had increased when refugees from the Hundred Year's War swarmed into

Brittany. The town became a real stronghold. The defenses of the city gates were doubled by outposts or boulevards: the **Portes Mordelaises**, the only ones still standing, today help us envision the town's military past as well as the solemn entry of the dukes when they went to be consecrated in the cathedral.

Near the Vilaine river, construction on **Saint-Germain**, the parish church of the rich cloth merchants, continued throughout the 15th century and well beyond. At the beginning of the 16th century the sole gigantic opening in flamboyant Gothic style on the west facade, not here visible, adopted a formula already employed in the city around 1494 in the chapel of the *Hôpital Saint-Yves*, a sumptuous ducal institution. The gable of the south transept, finished in 1610, is a good example of how difficult it was to adapt the new formal concepts of superposed orders to the Gothic mass. Finally, in the 17th century a series of chapels was set around the entire south flank, respecting the original character of the building. Inside, the projected stone vaulting was never realized: because of the instability of the terrain, the only solution was a

This vast ensemble, created in 1750 by the architect of the king, Jacques Gabriel. reconciles the Baroque of its broad central hemicycle and the ridged dome with the severity of the pavilions and the central niche.

Facing page, above: the Palais Saint-Georges, a typical example of 17th-cent. architecture with its large pavilion roof and alternating semicircular and triangular pediments over the windows. Below: the limestone pavilions in eclectic style in the garden of Thabor, flanked by vast hothouses with metal domes, created in 1863 by the architect Martenot.

very high paneled ceiling which allowed a tall window, identical to the one on the west facade, to be installed in the apse. Reused 16th-century stained glass elements in the window of the south transept narrate stories from the life of the Virgin and of Christ: sole survivors of the flourishing school of master glass-workers in Rennes. The present high altar and the baldaquin were ordered in 1784 for the cathedral of Saint-Malo.

Rue Saint-Georges, to the east of the center that was rebuilt after the fire of 1720, and the old canons' quarter to the west, still have several half-timbered houses. In the *Rue Saint-Guillaume*, at the cathedral apse, two semi-detached prebendary houses are dedicated to St. Michael (the one on the left) and to St. Sebastian (on the right). Despite the fact that the structure with its decided overhang and with sculptured Gothic leaves in the molding is still basically medieval, the presence of the small columns that underscore the uprights are already early Renaissance and indicate a construction date of around 1500. At the end of the 16th century, after Brittany once more became part of France, Parliament established its head-

quarters in Rennes. In order to house the members of this assembly when it was in session, the carpenters of Rennes constructed timber-frame "apartment" houses that were four or five stories high. The tall frame buildings set against the ramparts in *Place du Champ-Jacquet* give us a sampling of the different types of half-timbering then in use: herring bone, St. Andrew's cross, and squared diamonds, marvelously set together, creating an inexpensive decor. Even so, half-timbered architecture was on the way out as early as 1650. The dictates of fashion and the municipal edicts led to the disappearance of the cantilevered upper stories, as well as a cruder construction method in which the pieces of wood of varying diameters were masked by a layer of plaster. After its hour of glory, half-timbered architecture was gradually replaced by stone. Nevertheless the creativity of the carpenters of Rennes was given free rein in the upper parts: pavilion roofs, keel roofs, double deckers covered the dormers and the stair wells of the mansions built for the members of parliament along the Place des Lices.

The Palais du Parlement, articulated by a rigorous classic order. The square, dating to 1936, accentuates the effect of its mass.

Facing page: general view and detail of the ceiling of the Grand Chambre, a vast highly decorative composition which can barely be taken in at a single glance.

Palais du Parlement

At the beginning of the 17th century the construction of a vast palace was undertaken in order to provide the Parliament of Brittany with a setting worthy of this sovereign court — the superior court of justice and the place where royal edicts were recorded. The site chosen was in the Ville-Neuve, on land belonging to the convent of the Cordeliers, and this shifted the center of town eastwards, for some time. The present building represents two different tendencies in French art in the first half of the 17th century: the Palais itself, conceived by the architect Germain Gautier as a square around a court, with pavilions and multiple branches, clearly remains within the tradition of French architecture. Salomon de Brosse, Marie de Medici's architect, added a unified facade on the front, with Ionic pilasters on the lower floor, completely new in style. Even so, the great roof above the Italianate balustrade is pure French. In the inner court the harmony of brick and stone recalls the great Parisian ensembles of Louis XIII. The palace however is particularly striking for the extraordinary luxury of the interior decor, all too little known. A loggia-like staircase leads to the first floor. It wa built in 1725 by Jacques Gabriel, architect to the king, when the Place Royale in front was redesigned. This new entrance replaced Salomon de

Brosse's great staircase, which up to then had occupied the center of the main facade, and the terrace. The most striking of the state rooms, the *Grande-Chambre*, was decorated under the direction of Charles Erard, one of the greatest Parisian decorators of his time, reponsible for the great ensembles of the Louvre and the Tuileries under the Regency of Anne of Austria. The extraordinary ceiling which combines the Italian concept of coffers containing paintings with the French tradition of a flat ceiling is in fact suspended on an invisible metal armature. It was carved in Paris and sent via the Loire and then the Vilaine to Rennes. Around the room Gobelin tapestries of the year 1900, designed by Edouard Toulouze, evoke the high points in the history of Brittany and harmoniously complete this sumptuous decoration.

In the city, the rebuilding of the facade of the **cathedral of Saint-Pierre** was begun in 1560 and finished a century later. The marvelous array of clustered columns, the narrowness of the tall nave, alien to the Baroque esthetics of the period, were in fact the result of an adaptation to the framework of the precedent Gothic building. The latter was itself replaced entirely after 1784 with a new structure designed by Crucy, architect from Nantes. The interior, with its rows of columns, originally all in white stone, was one of the most spectacular examples of neo-Classic architecture in early 19th-century France. Around

Church of Saint-Germain. Above: the extension of gables on the south side. Left: the interior of the nave towards the apse.

1860 the canons of taste had changed, and this simplicity seemed cold: a sumptuous decor of stucco and gold, with painting and stained glass transformed Crucy's church into a Roman basilica, rather overpowering in its decoration.

Inside and outside the walls, a ring of convents separated the town from its suburbs until the 19th century and made any allover reconstruction impossible. To the east, the **Palais Saint-Georges**, the only vestige of a Benedictine Abbey (for women), is a good example of the wealth and importance of the religious orders in Rennes until the end of the Ancien Régime. The long porticoed structure built overlooking the river Vilaine around 1670 bears the name of the Abbess Madeleine de La Fayette. It is the work of the architect Pierre Corbineau, from Lavalle, who also designed the Abbey Palace of Saint-Melaine in Rennes and a great number of Baroque reredos throughout Brittany. In December 1720 a gigantic fire destroyed almost all of the wooden houses in the center of the town. The provincial military engineer, Isaac Rebelin, furnished a project for reconstruction based on a strict orthogonal plan, with two squares in a hierarchy: one in front of the Palais du Parlement, the **Place du Palais**, was to glorify the Sun King; the other, shifted towards the southwest, called **Place Neuve**. New edifices built entirely of stone, on hollow vaults, their heights and facades unified in design, were planned to line either side of the streets laid out at right angles. However the authoritarianism of Rebelin roused the wrath of the citizens of Rennes and the first architect to the king, Jacques Gabriel, had to be called in for arbitration. He proved conciliatory with regards to the private houses and proposed a variety of modules for the facades. It was thus easier for him to impose his project for the Place Royale in front of the Palais and build a new monument on the Place Neuve, which he enclosed in an ample curve, the *Hôtel de Ville* and the *Tour de l'Horloge*, with a statue of Louis XV in a niche below and place for the Presidial. This complex completely modified the aspect of the town and for a long time left the mark of a rather severe classic style. The new buildings stretch out their uniform rows of granite arcades, differing only in the treatment of the openings above with their iron railings, along the streets that were rebuilt in the 18th century.

In the 19th century the town extended first towards the east. The demolition of the old Chapel of the Cordeliers, Place du Palais, of the church of the Abbaye Saint-Georges, near the gate of the same name, made it possible to lay out a new entrance to the city and connect it directly to the suburb of Paris. The elegant quarter began to spring up at this time — first around the Square de la Motte, then south of the former garden of the Benedictines of Saint-Melaine. The latter, the **Thabor**, was to be completely redesigned around 1860 by the Bulhër brothers. Finally in 1844 the course of the river Vilaine was regulated, 120 years after Robelin's project. The newly-built embankments provided the occasion for new monumental complexes.

In an ambitious program the University (Palais Universitaire) built between 1849 and 1856, associated the faculties of Rennes and the Museums of Fine Art, Archaeology and Natural History. In addition to its remarkable drawing cabinet, the **Musée des Beaux-Arts** is particularly rich in paintings which are grouped in broad periods, and include the *St. Luke Painting the Virgin* by Maerten Van Heemskerck, a *Perseus and Andromeda* by Veronese from the collections of Louis XIV. The many 17th-century paintings of the French school include the *Newborn Babe*, by Georges de La Tour, a masterpiece of French Caravaggism, a *Virgin au Verre* by Matheieu Le Nain, two rare canvases by Lubin Baugin, including a perfect *Still Life with Gallettes*, as well as an important group of Dutch paintings.

After World War II, material dealing with the history of Brittany and that evoking the ways and customs of the Bretons was united in a single museum. The pride of the collections of the **Musée de Bretagne** is without doubt the statue of a young goddess, in bronze, discovered at the

Facade and choir of the cathedral of Saint-Pierre.

12

beginning of the 20th century near a Gallo-Roman temple in Finistère. The crested helmet of Greek type she wears on her wavy hair identifies her as a Celtic version of Athena-Minerva, called *Brigit* in the Irish manuscripts of the Early Middle Ages.

In sharp contrast to this esthetic and documentary evolution, the marvelous *gala bed* made by the Rennes atelier of Adolphe Coignerai for the Exposition Universelle of 1900 exemplifies the attempt at a renewal in furniture design which began in the 1870s. One of the most representative aspects of this movement was the "*mobilier a personnages*" of which the bed is an exceptional example. The superabundance of spindles assembled into a wheel or semi-wheel design was also found in the same period on the *lits-close* (cuboard beds) of folk furniture in the south of Brittany. On the other hand, the form itself of this piece of furniture, its iconography, and the extraordinarily sophisticated sculpture, practically a tour de force, are all in fact alien to the tradition of Breton furniture.

Facing page: The Musée des Beaux-Arts, formerly Palais Universitaire. Above: the facade which, in its neo-classic version, recalls the earlier Parlement. Below: the large gallery remodelled after the war with ceiling illumination.

Two works preserved in the Musée de Bretagne. Right: head of Brigit-Minerva discovered in Dineault at the foot of the Monts d'Arrée. Below: Gala bed (by Adolphe Coignerai, Rennes, 1900) where the high relief scene refers to the episode of the battle of Trente, in the War of Succession in Brittany in the 14th century.

The castle and the town seen from the northwest. In the background, the spire of the church of Saint-Martin, rebuilt at the end of the 19th century.

Facing page, above: the castle, the porte d'Embas and the half-timbered houses of the 17th and 18th centuries, clustered at the foot of the ramparts. Below: the inner court of the castle with, on the left, the old covered staircase leading to the grand logis and, on the right, the tall structure of the châtelet.

VITRE

An outpost of Brittany, Vitré soon entered the sphere of influence of her powerful neighbors. The lords of Vitré, who were also barons of Laval, were allied to the Montmorency and in imitation of the Duke and of the King of France, their joint sovereigns, they adopted an adroit policy of alternating alliances, quite typical of the feudal world. Around 1060 Robert de Vitré transferred the **castle** to an inaccessible spur between two valleys that could easily be defended. Of the large edifice built then, perhaps similar in plan to the square Norman keep, nothing remains today except a fine Romanesque gate, in the court of the castle to the right of the châtelet. In 1239 the last daughter of the baron of Vitré married the baron of Laval. The destiny of the two towns became one, above and beyond any borders, and the new lord reinforced his castle of Vitré with the present triangular wall which fused with the form of the spur. The village around the castle became a real town and surrounded itself with ramparts of blue-black schist which survived up to the 19th century. Today the north side, intact, still dominates the valley of the Vilaine.

In the 14th and 15th centuries various marriages brought the lords of Laval-Vitré important holdings in Haute Bretagne: Châteaubriant, Tinteniac, Montfort, and Rais. . . Construction work done on the castle at various times led to its present picturesque silhouette. The imposing entrance *châtelet* of around 1380 is a tall edifice of four levels joined by a polygonal tower-staircase. The prime scope of this impressive structure was symbolic, meant to proclaim the power of the lord of Vitré to the visitor. The other building, no longer extant, joined the châtelet to the Tour de la Madeleine: the numerous elements of comfort inside, including a stove and many rooms for diverse uses, give us an insight into the requirements of this refined court. The wall was also reinforced at the three corners by strong towers, which doubled as defense and dwelling place. At the end of the 15th century another edifice was built along the north front where the Town Hall now stands. Built on arcading, the (first) floor was turned into a communication gallery modelled on the one in Blois, ancestor of our modern lobby. On the southwest front, lastly, a charming little apse, sculptured in micaceous chalk, added to the oratory tower in 1513 by Guy XVI de Laval, symbolizes the arrival of the

Rue Baudrairie.

Facing page: two views of the church of Notre-Dame, the most successful type of church with its rows of gables, in Haute Bretagne.

Renaissance in Vitré.

In the Middle Ages Vitré soon became a flourishing commercial town. An intense cottage industry of weaving provided a livelihood for entire families in the surrounding countryside. These famous pieces of cloth were exported by the local merchants throughout Europe: in close association with those of Saint-Malo, they grouped together in 1472 into a guild of Over-Seas Merchants, under the protection of the Virgin of the Annunciation. A number of old houses in the town also proudly display, in imitation of the coat of arms, the trademark of the merchant, a personal emblem and a guaranty of his product. Some of the rich houses of the 15th century, in delicately molded and carved half timbering, rival the aristocratic dwellings in their luxury. They consisted of two detached buildings, one on the street and the other at the back of the court, joined by a gallery. *Rue Baudrairie*, whose name (baudrier-baldrick, shoulder belt) calls to mind the working of leather, has maintained the ambience of these prosperous times intact and timber-work houses with corbelled facades jostle each other. In the *Rue Notre-Dame* and the *Rue Poterie* a permanent display of merchandise was held under the "porched" houses.

In the heart of the town, opposite the old market halls which no longer exist, the **church of Notre-Dame**, rebuilt between 1420 and 1550, expresses the pride of the bourgeoisie of Vitré. Its vast quadrilateral, surrounded by a multiplicity of gables and articulated by spires, as frequently found in Haute Bretagne, shelters a nave, two side aisles and, on either side, a row of chapels, commissioned by confraternities or notables of the town and enriched with statues, altarpieces and stained glass. The south facade is a fine variation on the repertory of Breton flamboyant Gothic architecture. In the center, an external pulpit grafted onto a buttress is a rare example of this form in the west of France, together with the one of Saint-Lô in Normandy.

Further on down the street, *Place du Marchix, Rue de Paris* and *Rue de Embas*, with various town mansions of the 16th and 17th centuries, attest to the emergence in Vitré of an authentic urban patrician class which rose from the merchants. The decline in the cloth trade in the 18th century was to mark the beginning of a long period of lethargy for the town from which it did not reawaken until the middle of the 19th century, when the railroad passed through and drastically altered the nature of the town.

Above: the castle seen from the church of Saint-Leonard with, in the foreground, the "old town" and its half-timbered houses. On the left: the tower of Coigny.

FOUGERES

Recent archaeological digs have brought to light the traces of a first wooden keep built in the 10th century on the northwest point of the schistose rock. The present **fortress** complex that spreads out over more than two hectares provides us with a veritable lesson in military architecture, ranging from the 12th to the end of the 15th century. The barons of Fougères reinforced the original castle with a vast wall which embraced the form of the rock and barred the entrance at the narrowest point of the curve. Of the large edifice then built against the south wall nothing remains but ruins. An industrial town soon developed: below the castle, another bend of the Nançon was occupied by the tanners, fullers and weavers. The elegant **church of Saint-Sulpice**, rebuilt in the 15th century, has two rare altarpieces in carved granite of the 1500s: one of them, offered by a confraternity of tanners, lets us envision the prosperity this craft brought. In the middle of the 13th century the De Lusignan family began to enlarge the defense system of the **castle** of Fougères, bringing it to its present size. At either end the wall was reinforced by towers, the protection of the entrance was doubled and, above all, an extraordinary hydraulic system was installed. A succession of meres made it possible to hold the assailants at bay in the north, to keep the

water level in the moats to the south at a constant level, and finally to provide water for the mills of the manor, protected by the wall of Bourg-Neuf which climbed up the slope of the hill towards the east. The new town itself also became an element of subsidiary defense for the castle. With its imposing fortress and the wealth provided by its commercial activities, Fougères was courted throughout the Middle Ages both by the kings of France and the dukes of Brittany. The pointed silhouette of the 15th-century **belfry** which still dominates the upper town, near the old gate of Vitré, the **Hôtel de Ville** (town hall) of 1535, one of the oldest in Brittany, are still the living symbols of the franchises and the liberties which the town then enjoyed. Damaged by several fires in the course of the 18th century, the Upper Town was progressively rebuilt in line with plans furnished by Jacques Gabriel, architect to the king. Various aristocratic dwellings, including the elegant **Hôtel de la Belinaye** with its concave facade, bear the mark of his severe style. In the Rue Nationale, also perfectly realigned and rebuilt at the time in the fine golden brown granite of Saint-Marc-le-Blanc, one sole house with timber framing remains as a reminder of the old town: it contains a **Musée Emmanuel de la Villéon**, one of the last impressionist painters. A bit further on, the church of **Saint-Léonard** attests to the wealth of the city in the 15th and 16th centuries. Its original entrance was on the west, opposite to where it is now.

Right: the ensemble of the castle outpost. Below: the church of Saint-Léonard, founded in the 11th century and rebuilt in the 14th century. The gabled chapels seen here were added in the 15th and 16th centuries.

COMBOURG

Around 1025, Junkeneus, archbishop and count of Dol, decided to put his brother Rivallon in charge of the defenses of the eastern border of his territory. An initial earthen fort, southeast of the present mere, already controlled the passage of the ancient Roman travelers from Rennes to Aleth (now Saint-Servan). Before long, doubtless in the 12th century, the site of the castle was transferred to the northwest. The northeast tower of the castle, the oldest, dates to the beginning of the 13th century and the keep, originally isolated, was accessible only on the first floor. At the end of the 14th century the seignory of Combourg passed by marriage to the powerful family of Chateaugiron-Malestroit, which had a large building added on the south, fortified with two towers. In line with a general revision of the strongholds ordered by Duc Pierre II in the middle of the 15th century, the quadrilateral was closed off on the north by a strong tower and a second edifice. Around 1760, Rene-Auguste de Chateaubriand acquired the seignory of Combourg. The father of the famous author had recuperated the family fortunes thanks to a flourishing maritime commerce. The old fortress contained the dreams and nightmares of the man who was to write *Mémoires d'outre-tombe*. Around 1875 the moat which surrounded the fortress complex on three sides was filled in when the Bülher brothers replaced it with an English garden.

Left: the machicolated castle towers, typical of the Breton fortifications in the 15th century. Below: general view of the castle.

Panorama from the south-west.

MONT-SAINT-MICHEL

The discovery of Mont-Saint-Michel is at first sight that of a place. The astonishing silhouette of a pyramidical rock rises up in the middle of a bay that seems deserted, its height doubled by the buildings and the abbey church that crown it.

The monument is the negation of its environment, and therefore the relationship between the two is close. On this mythical site, legend frequently gets the better of reality, so that reality ceases to be reality. The statue of the archangel is a link between the material world and the sky. At its feet, the ideal society of the Middle Ages has been represented: the clergy at the top, knights on the ramparts, laborers in the village. As soon as you leave this order, the bay is there with its mobile sands, image of death, and the tide surges in over the endless expanse of the strands twice daily.

The awareness that this immense space is an extraordinary place of life and the site of intense biological activity is of relatively recent date. The point of departure for organized crossings of the bay on foot is generally Genets. Joining them is the best way of discovering the Mont in depth. For centuries this is how the pilgrims arrived, on foot, from the north. If you are unable to take advantage of this occasion, at least take the time to go around the rock on the sand. It is an indispensable prelude to the visit of the monument and the sole means by which the power of its military architecture, too often overshadowed by the presence and prestige of the monastery, can strike home.

To reach the abbey from the strand, one must pass through the **village**, which presents today's tourist with the hotels, restaurants and souvenir shops once offered to

General view of the abbey church: the Romanesque nave and the flamboyant Gothic choir.

Facing page: le Mont-Saint-Michel, the isle of Tombelaine and the bay at high tide.

the pilgrims. A narrow street opens up after having passed three fortified gates. Climbing up the south and east sides of the rock, the village still has a few old houses, including the one called of the *artichoke* (artichauts), which forms a bridge over the street, and that of the *Licorne*.

A long climb leads to the **abbey**. There, from the 8th to the 16th century, men built sanctuary on sanctuary and all the buildings the monks needed to sing praise to God. Tradition says that the archangel Michael appeared to the Bishop of Avranches Aubert in 708, enjoining him to build an oratory here on the rock. Since then, Mont-Saint-Michel has been a pilgrimage site, which developed considerably after the duke of Normandy entrusted it to Benedictine monks in 966.

The nature of the terrain, a pointed rock, approximately conical, obliged the later master builders to use original expedients. As early as the beginning of the 11th century, the will to erect a great *abbey church* in the traditional cross plan made it necessary to build a series of crypts all around the summit of the rock, meant to provide a level support for the four arms of the cross, choir, transept and nave. Only half of the church thus rests directly on the granite.

The first **convent buildings** erected in the second half of the 11th century had to rise tier on tier in three levels instead of spreading out around a cloister, as in all the other monasteries. This principle of tiers was maintained throughout the history of the construction, and finds its apotheosis in the "Merveille", built in the first quarter of the 13th century and crowned by the cloister and the refectory which are, with the Salle des Chevaliers, the most famous parts of the abbey.

The Carolingian sanctuary, the Romanesque Monastery and the Gothic Merveille were completed in the 15th century by the choir of the abbey church, in flamboyant Gothic style, the most formidable demonstration of the development of medieval architecture still extant.

Above: Cancale, view of the port of La Houle. Left: the cathedral of Saint-Samson in Dol-de-Bretagne.

CANCALE

Situated west of the bay of Mont-Saint-Michel, Cancale is a charming small fishing port that invites one to stop. The old fishermen's quarter of **La Houle** crouches at the foot of its rocky cliff. Tourists will find souvenir shops and restaurants with oyster specialties here. The flat bay, which permits the waters to recede several kilometers from the coast at low tide, has favored oyster farming and the oyster pens seem to stretch out endlessly. At the top, a village has grown up around the **church of Saint-Méen**, a vast neo-Gothic structure of the 19th century with a tower that serves as belvedere. It can be reached from the point of departure of the pedestrian itinerary of the guard walk. After the *Pointe des Crolles* which dominates the port up to the *Pointe du Grouin*, one can continue along the coast for about seven kilometers among the maritime pines and the flowering gorse with views over the *Rocher de Cancale*, the *Châtelier* and the *Ile des Rimains* and its fort with, in the distance if the weather is clear, the Normandy coast of Cotentin. With *Port-Mer* and its beach, Cancale still combines the attractions of a family resort with various activities.

Above: Pointe du Grouin and the tip of the Ile des Landes.
Right: the menhir of Champ-Dolent, near Dol-de-Bretagne.

DOL-DE-BRETAGNE

The small town of Dol-de-Bretagne can pride itself on having the purest example of Breton Gothic — the **cathedral of Saint-Samson**. One should not be discouraged by the austere facade, disfigured and incomplete. The great interior fabric of the 13th century with a flat chevet pierced by a magnificent stained-glass window still calls to mind the pretensions of the bishops of Dol who insisted on supremacy over their Breton suffragans.
A few kilometers from Dol stands the enigmatic **menhir of Champ-Dolent** which is reckoned among the most important in Brittany. All this hinterland of transition between Brittany and Normandy is thus charged with history.

POINTE DU GROUIN

A wild outpost towards the open sea and the *Chausey Isles*, the Pointe du Grouin offers a magnificent panorama of the bay of Mont-Saint-Michel. Right opposite, the rocky spur of the *Ile des Landes* shelters one of the most important colonies of marine birds on this coast. Towards Cancale the *Ile des Rimains* crowned by an old fort stands out on the horizon while landwards, on clear days, one can get a glimpse of *Mont-Dol*, the only high point in this flat land.

Above: panorama of the town: the
Vaubin basin and the ramparts.

Left, above: panorama of the cité d'Alet;
center: the Vauban basin and the
ramparts; below: view towards the Fort
National from the top of the Great Keep
of the Castle.

SAINT-MALO

Saint-Malo looks as if it had risen up out of the past even though, with the exception of the ramparts, the town was actually largely rebuilt after 1944. Reconstruction was however carried out as faithfully as possible. The town bears the name of a monk, Machlow or Malo, who arrived in the 6th century from what is now Wales. The prosperity of "Saint-Malo-de l'Isle", as it was called, began in the 16th century, shortly before Jacques Cartier set sail from here for Canada (1534). Shrewd merchants, the citizens of Malo were also privateers of the king in times of war: Duguay-Trouin and, later, Surcouf, were the most famous. But a whole pleiad of authors, philosophers and intellectuals were also native to Saint-Malo, including Chateaubriand, Lamennais, Mauper-

tuis, La Mettrie and Broussais. The prestige of these outstanding men, all born within these walls, is moreover accompanied by one of the loveliest maritime sites in France. All its beauty can best be appreciated by making a tour of the **ramparts**, also an ideal site from which to observe the quality of an urban architecture that drew inspiration from the late 17th-century military engineers. Begun in the 12th century, the ramparts were enlarged in four different stages during the course of the 18th century, providing the "Messieurs de Saint-Malo" with a site on which to build their most beautiful dwellings. The spire of the cathedral, also restored, indicates the heart of the city.

The **castle** of Saint-Malo was begun in 1424 when Duc

Facing page, above: view of the town from the Great Keep of the castle; below: statue of Chateaubriand and the Saint-Vincent gates.

Above: the Quic-en-Groigne tower of the castle. Right: the house of Anne of Brittany.

Jean V of Brittany gave orders for the construction of the *Gros-Donjon* (great keep) which now houses the Musée d'Histoire de la Ville. Duc François II added the *Tour Générale* after 1475 and his daughter Anne of Brittany insisted on completing this complex despite the protests of the citizens of Malo. *Quic-en-Groigne, ainsi sera, c'est mon plaisir*, she is said to have answered. Ever since then, the large tower adjacent to the *Petit-Donjon* of the 14th century bears the curious name of "Quic-en-Groigne". In the inner court, the former barracks building of the 18th century houses the Town Hall. In 1590, the citizens of Malo took possession of their castle and for four years declared an "Independent Republic". The standard of the city floating at the top of the *Gros Donjon* still recalls those ancient liberties. From the *Tourelles de Guet* there is a magnificent panorama of the reconstructed town. Near the castle, a few historical houses still stand, such as the one where Chateaubriand was born (he now rests, as was his desire, on the neighboring isle of Grand Bé) and the charming house of the duchess Anne, Cour La Hussaye.

Above: the port and the Solidor tower. Left: another view of the tower, which houses the Musée du Long-Cours Cap-Hornier.

SAINT SERVAN SUR MER

Nowadays Saint-Servan-sur-Mer officially depends on Saint-Malo. For all that the ancient Gallo-Roman center of Aleth is in the territory of Saint-Servan, and vestiges of the cathedral and the city walls can still be seen. The most remarkable of its monuments is the **Tour Solidor** which stands on a small cape in the estuary of the Rance and over which it seems to be keeping watch. The construction was in effect ordered by Duc Jean IV of Brittany, shortly before 1384, to subject the inhabitants of Malo to his authority. It contains the highly interesting *Musée de Cap-Horniers*, dedicated to the windjammers whose crews were recruited along the entire coast. Small-scale models, nautical instruments, maps and objects made on board or brought from far-distant ports of call let us relive the adventure of these voyages around the world on the great long-distance sailing vessels. From the fine promenade of the **cité d'Aleth** on its green promontory opposite Dinard and Saint-Malo, there are some fine vistas over the estuary barred by the dam and *hydroelectric station* of the Rance. In adopting the traditional technique of the sea mills, these waterworks, inaugurated in 1966, produce more than 500 million kwh, using the tidal currents that are stronger here than anywhere else in continental Europe.

View of the rooftops of the old town of Dinan from the Tour de l'Horloge.

DINAN

The etymology of the name Dinan which first appeared in the 11th century designates an eminence or hilltop suitable for defense. But Dinan was still nothing but the feudal motte of a noble family when the soldiers of William the Conqueror besieged it, as seen in the famous Bayeux Tapestry. The apportionment effectuated among the successors in 1123 gives us an idea of the importance of the town which was at the time comprised of two parishes. Crossroads for the land routes towards Rennes, Normandy, the Armorican West, and the sea via Rance towards Saint-Malo and the coast, Dinan was one of the liveliest cities of the old duchy of Bretagne, specialized in the cloth industry. Moreover, at the end of the 13th century the Duc de Bretagne obtained control of this stronghold. While there was an endless succession of sieges until the arrival of the French at the end of the 15th century, Dinan managed to escape destruction. Together with Vitré, it thus remains one of the Breton cities where the mark of the Middle Ages is strongest and is one of the finest towns of art and history in the region. Its **town walls**, whose circuit is still almost intact, enclosed a rather vast area with room for both the townspeople and the religious establishments. Surrounded by an ensemble of picturesque wooden houses, the **Tour de l'Horloge** rises up above the close-set roofs. A fascinating panorama can be had from the top. But arriving in Dinan by the great viaduct is just as exciting. The town, firmly planted on its plateau, dominates the deep green valley and rises up before us magically with its walls, towers and belfries. The first thing that catches our eye is the tower, unfinished, alas, of the **church of Saint-Malo**. This structure was originally situated outside the town walls and was rebuilt inside after 1490 as indicated in the fine inscription in Gothic letters on one of the pillars in the choir. This reconstruction has bequeathed us the remarkable apse in flamboyant Gothic style dating to this period and which can best be seen from the courtyard of the former Couvent des Cordeliers where we can admire, in passing, the fine granite portal. Dinan was also a town dear to Bertrand Du Guesclin who here engaged in a famous duel with Sir Thomas of Canterbury on the square that now bears his name and where his statue stands.

The **basilica of Saint-Sauveur** was founded around 1120 by a lord of Dinan who, it is said, had made a vow to build a church on his return from the crusades. This also explains the originality of the decoration of the still extant Romanesque parts, but the three arches of the main portal recall more directly the art of the southwest of

France and in particular Notre-Dame-la-Grande in Poitiers. The ensemble which consists of this facade and the entire south side remains on the whole exceptional for Brittany where no other monument of this period is of such high quality. The great window over the portal and the entire north part of the building date to the end of the 15th century. The choir was begun in 1507 as witnessed by an inscription similar to that in the church of Saint-Malo, which inspired it, but with a decoration in the chapels which more surely heralds the Renaissance. The tower, begun in the 17th century, received its curious wood and slate belfry in the following century. In 1810, the tombstone that covered the grave where the heart of Du Guesclin had been buried as he desired, was transferred to this church, which also contains interesting furnishings.

The famous gabled houses with their cantilevered porticoes and half timbering, leaning at all angles against each other, stand along the **Place de l'Apport** and the main thoroughfare of the medieval city. Most of them date to the 15th and 16th centuries. The facades of some of them

Left: facade of the church of Saint-Sauveur. Below: detail of the Romanesque portal.

Facing page, above: the Tour de l'Horloge; below: old half-timbered houses with porches.

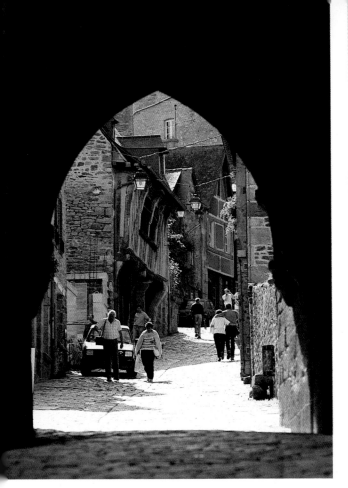

Jerzual Gate.

Booths near the Tour de l'Horloge.

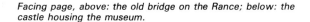

Facing page, above: the old bridge on the Rance; below: the castle housing the museum.

have a sort of bay enclosed in glass which, to a certain extent, recalls a ship's castle. Some of these "showcases" also exist in the old Saint-Malo. Merchants and artisans set up shop under the porches. One can imagine how crowded this part of the town must have been when the heavy wagons going down or coming up from the Rance encountered each other on this road, the only one before the construction of the large viaduct in 1852. Ever since the 15th century the **Tour d'Horloge** has been a landmark in the heart of the city. Its elegant Gothic portal opens onto the street of the same name. Godmother of the great bell which strikes the hours was the duchess Anne, but it had to be recast in 1906. *Place Du Guesclin* can be reached by following a passageway recently installed in old courtyards where pleasant covered booths have been built. Further on is the **Château**, which houses a museum at present being renovated. Contemporary to the Tour Solidor in Saint-Servan, the *keep* was begun in 1382 for Duc Jean IV of Brittany. There are flour floors of magnificent rooms and a chapel. The collections relate the history of Dinan and its land. On the other hand the remarkable "gisants" (recumbant tomb figures) of the 14th century are to be found on the ground floor of the *Tour de Coëtquen*. From the viaduct there is a plunging view from above over the valley of the Rance and the *port district* of Dinan, now used only by pleasure boats and launches for excursions to Saint-Malo. From the Apport one can descend the picturesque *Rue du Jerzual* all the way down to the old bridge. Artisans are attempting to bring this once active district back to life. The street, oddly closed off by an ogival gate situated at the bottom of an old watch tower, also has lovely wooden houses which have been marvelously restored. After this long descent, the quays and the tow-lines invite strolling. Nothing is more charming in effect than these shores of the Rance, as Chateaubriand so brilliantly wrote!

Facing page, above: the beach of the Ecluse and the Pointe de la Malouine in Dinard; below: the Pointe du Décollé at Saint-Lunaire.

The fort of La Latte.

DINARD

On the left bank of the estuary of the Rance, Dinard offers a surprising contrast to the corsair city on the opposite shore. Here neither history nor monuments, nothing but a relatively recent settlement comprised of villas, hotels and houses. Actually Dinard was created shortly after 1850 thanks to the infatuation of rich English families who built the first villas on its spits of land. The site attracted people in the public eye: writers, politicians, aristocrats, artists. Despite the change in clientele and in taste that has taken place since then, modern Dinard has retained its peculiar charm. The beauty of the site together with its luxuriant vegetation makes it easy to see why. Opposite Saint-Servan and the Tour Solidor, sheltered from the prevailing winds, the **Promenade du Clair de Lune** which dominates the bay of the Prieuré is one of the most charming spots in this resort town. You have to be there on a lovely summer evening, when the flower beds are illuminated and mood music fills the air. Like all seaside resorts worthy of the name, Dinard also has its casino, the Palais d'Emeraude, a center for congresses, and a heated swimming pool. These establishments open directly onto the large **Plage de l'Ecluse** whose fine sands stretch out as far as the Pointe du Moulinet and the Pointe de la Malouine which together with La Vicomté form one of the loveliest districts of Dinard.

LA COTE D'EMERAUDE

Saint-Lunaire, with its *Pointe du Décollé*, offers what may be the most complete lookout point of the Emerald Coast. The name dates to the beginning of the century and is due to the way the ever-changing skies, the algae, the currents, and the green trees clinging to the jagged rocks despite the wind are reflected in the water. Towards the east the *Malouine peninsula* with its outposts of fortified islets, Bés, Cézembre and, closer, Harbourg. On the west is the *Pointe de la Garde-Guérin*, in Saint-Briac, the *Ile Agot* and the *Ile des Hébihens*.
Fort La Latte also lies right on the ocean, near *Cap Fréhel*, and the way it blends into the wild cliffs in pink granite where marine birds nest is striking. Begun in the Middle Ages by the founding family of the princes of Monaco, the fortress with its round towers was improved under Vauban who furnished it with cannons with which to fight the aggression of Saint-Malo.

The monument with Athena watching over Ernest Renan, Place du Martray.

Facing page, above: two views of the half-timbered facades on Rue Ernest Renan and Rue de La Chalotais; below: the house of Ernest Renan, now a museum.

TREGUIER

Jaudy. . . Guindy. In Tréguier everything begins like a somewhat old-fashioned nursery rhyme. The past reigns supreme at the confluence of rivers with the pretty names, Guindy-Jaudy.

An estuary town, of old facing the high seas like its Breton sisters, the piers of Tréguier no longer see the sand pushed up by the brave coastal vessels at the end of their course. Pleasure boats however still find a place to rest their hulls throughout the year.

Half-timbered houses of the 15th and 16th centuries enliven the central square of Martray, whose name recalls a cemetery that once stood right next to the cathedral. At the back of Rue Renan two square towers are what remain of a gate of the former city walls.

The **city hall** is installed in the former bishop's palace. The Psalette, the Chantrerie call to mind the children and the cantors who animated the liturgy in the cathedral when it still had its bishop. Rue de La Chalotais and Rue Gambetta, where the **Hôtel-Dieu** can be seen. A 13th-century parlor, a 15th and 17th-century chapel are still part of the domain of the Augustine Hospitallers. Rue Colvestre, arched portal of 1438 appertaining to the medieval bishop's palace which once stood here. On the Place du Martray, south of the cathedral stands the *statue of Ernest Renan* (author of a rational "Vie de Jesus"). He is shown seated, holding his cane, weighed down with years. Behind this native son of Tréguier the sculptor Jean Boucher has set the Greek goddess Pallas Athena, her helmet on her head, triumphant and proudly brandishing the laurel branch of immortality and glory. A museum has been set up in **Renan's house**, where the writer's mother had a grocery shop, in the street which now bears her son's name. The room where Ernest lived as a child is on the third story. The bust, the letters, the manuscripts of this great man have been devoutly collected here together with the shawl of Henriette, his ever-attentive sister.

As at Saint-Pol, history here began with a Welsh monk.

Tugdual, then known as Tudy or Pabu, after wandering along the Quimper coast of Cornouaille, went up towards Tréguier where he was consecrated bishop around 540. The **cathedral**, a complex building, no longer has its original high facade. The towers are at the transept. In the *Hasting tower*, at the north, an odd Romanesque capital illustrates the biblical story of the daughters of Loth. On the south, the 15th-century tower was not terminated with its spire until 1785, under Monsignor Le Mintier, last bishop of Tréguier, after he had obtained 20,000 francs from the king, taken from the Paris lottery. The body of the church, begun in 1339, has a Gothic nave with a triforium. The tomb of St. Yves, patron saint of lawyers, in the aisle is a faithful copy made in 1890 of the one destroyed by the batallion of d'Etampes which occupied the building in 1794. The skull of the saint is in a reliquary in the treasury of the sacristy.

The *cloister*, a perfect space even though irregular in shape, dates to 1450. The tracery windows of the cathedral

Left: south side of the cathedral. Below: view of the nave, built in transitional Gothic style.

harmonize perfectly with the 48 arches in the three wings of the contiguous cloister. In a moderate flamboyant Gothic style, powerful cruciform piers alternate with the slender columns with their sober capitals. The porches are real museums of funerary art, with sarcophagi impressed with the form of the body, engraved funerary flagstones, set into the wall, and the reclining figure on his high tomb.

The epitaphs tell us of personages of long ago: E. Etiemble Morfoace, 1349; Eder, bishop of Saint-Brieuc, who died on December 24, 1431; Marguerite, rather mysterious, who died on April 10, 1463; and three reclining tomb figures sculptured in kersanton granite around 1640 by Roland Doré de Landerneaud, lords of the Bréhant and Bois-Boissel families, in the guise of musketeers.

In the center of the cloister, the 18th-century cross brought from Plouguielen in 1938 stands on the site of a statue of St. Yves.

Right: view of the choir rebuilt in 1339 in rayonnnant Gothic style. Below: the interior of the cloister and its fine flamboyant Gothic tracery.

Above: the rock of the Sentinelle in Port-Blanc. Left: the recently restored windmill of the Lande du Crac.

PORT BLANC

Port Blanc is first and foremost the **Sentinelle,** an oratory where the statue of the Virgin keeps watch over a marine landscape dotted with elongated archipelagos a stone's throw from the shore. In the past century more than one celebrity has settled here: in 1898, Anatole Le Bras, collector of legends, acquired the *Kerstellic* property; *Ty Chansonniou* was where Théodore Botrel sojourned before he settled in Pont-Aven; the *Ile Saint-Gildas* is the isle of Alexis Carrel, the great biologist who wrote *L'homme cet inconnu*; Lindbergh, who crossed the Atlantic in 1927 in the Spirit of Saint Louis, settled in *Illiec*, a cable's length away.

The **Moulin de la Lande du Crac** was restored in 1986. Rose walls rising from the schist, shingle roof. . . the great vanes testify to the fact that along the coast only the force of the tides could have been used to move the paddles of the sea mills. Wind was however also used to drive the mills.

PERROS-GUIREC

The fame of Perros, one of the best-known seaside resorts on the Côtes-du-Nord, derives from its beaches with their fine sand, *Trestraou* and *Trestrignel*.

The fine semi-Romanesque parish church is of pink granite. Not far off, **Notre-Dame de la Clarté**, a life-size marine ex-voto offered by the lord of Barac'h saved from a shipwreck, bestows pardon on the summer heights every August 15th. The porch topped by a secretairerie has a tympanum with the Pietà and one with the Annunciation, and under the vaults are the large statues of the Virgin, Saint Anne, Saint Peter and the Evangelists.

Inside, an altarpiece of the 17th century, old statues of St. Fiacre. St. Samson and St. Nicolas, patron of the mariners. On the walls hang the stations of the Cross painted by Maurice Denis in 1931. The painter, whose great stature has recently been revealed by the exhibitions of the Traouieros and the Musée de Morlaix, used to spend part of the year at Perros-Guirec.

Right: the chapel of Notre-Dame de la Clarté in Perros-Guirec.
Below: the vaulted porch of the chapel, a safe haven for the Virgin, St. Anne and a few fine Apostles.

Above: view of the harbor of Ploumanac'h. Left: the lighthouse on the western spit of the land.

Opposite: two views of the Côte de granit rose, between Perros-Guirec and Ploumanac'h.

PLOUMANAC'H AND THE COTE DE GRANIT ROSE

East of the commune of Perros-Guirec, the Pointe de Ploumanac'h consists of rocks where sea and wind erosion have sculptured modern pieces of abstract art: *Pors-Rolland, château du Diable, Squewel*. . .. The lighthouse, rebuilt after it had been destroyed on August 14, 1944, protects sailors from these marvelous pink rocks. Saint Guirec, the Welsh ''manac'h'' (monk), watches from his oratory seated on a stele from the Iron Age, evidence, with the pieces of electrum that were found, of a Celtic settlement. Close by the park of the ancient Fortress, conquered in 1594 by Royaux from the Ligueurs. The *château of Costaéres* numbers among its visitors the famous author of *Quo Vadis*, Seienkiewicz. Gustave Eiffel built his villa, Ker Awel, so appropriately named the abode of the wind, here.

Ploumanac'h, which was a town in the 14th century, still has some modest fishermen's houses, their solid walls loaded with souvenirs.

CHATEAU DE KERGRIST

Jean de Kergrist, the loveliest Christian name in Brittany — kergrist means house of Christ — began his château inland in 1537. Afterwards the main building was flanked by round towers, forming a U. The facades are articulated by large openings. For the Kergariou and the Barbier de Lescoet, the architect designed pediments with coats of arms and staircases leading down to the French gardens. 1792 also left its mark, for it is the date the last walls of the Ancien Régime in Brittany went up.

PLOUGONVEN

The artists who worked in Plougonven can be identified. The architect of most of the church, built in 1511, is the same Philippe Beaumanoir who created an original formula for the bell tower and the faceted chevet. The Calvary of 1554 is signed *Bastien et Henri Priget estoient Ymageurs* (sculptors). Yan Larc'haniec erected the three crosses in 1898, in the midst of a hundred figures which narrate the life of Christ, from His Birth to His Resurrection.

Left: the château of Kergrist in Ploubezce. Below: the parish close of Plougonven.

Above: the wet dock of Morlaix, dominated by the great viaduct. Right: the main street, the principal shopping center lined with old ''a lanterne'' houses.

MORLAIX

Morlaix, *Mons relaxus*, a mount deserted after the Gallo-Romans, a mount resettled in the Middle Ages on the hill of the Château, at the confluence of the Jarlot and the Queffleuth, straddles two lands, one might as well say two ethnic groups, Trégor and Léon, key to a vast region between the sea and the mountains.

Morlaix is tucked away at the back of the ford that opens onto the bay guarded over by the **Château du Taureau** which no longer strikes fear into the English. The port, occupied by pleasure boats, drawn up next to the landing stage below the long facade of the Tobacco Plant, is dominated by a large viaduct of fourteen arches, designed by the engineer Fenoux. In the old town, the streets are lined with old half-timbered houses decorated with sculpture.

Various churches are still standing: **Notre-Dame du Mur** and its vestiges; **Saint-Mathieu** with the cannon used against the league on its tower; **Saint-Melaine** built by the Beaumanoir five centuries ago. The municipal museum, one of the liveliest in Brittany, has been set up in the former Convent of the Jacobins.

Above: panorama of the town taken from the Kreisker bell tower. Left: facade of the cathedral, built in Norman style.

SAINT-POL-DE-LEON

Saint-Pol, the Breton *Castel Paol*, an old Roman fort is associated with St. Paul Aurelian, a Welsh evangelist of the 5th century, first bishop of Léon.

The 13th-century nave of the **cathedral**, in limestone from Caen, reveals its Norman Gothic origins, as does the silhouette of the steeple. The choir, 1431, contains a high altar in marble crowned by a palm-shaped ciborium in which the eucharist is kept and oak choir stalls (1504) on either side with carvings of plants and animals.

The tombs are lined up in the ambulatory, including that of Monsignor de la Marche, the last bishop, and a series of funerary urns, in the form of chapels, set on the *Etagères de la nuit*.

The neighboring spire of the **Chapelle du Kreisker**, 15th century, bears the mark of the English *perpendicular style*. An ambitious landmark, it calls to mind the vocation of a town formerly involved in traffic on the high seas, as far as the Americas.

Above: the château of Kerjean in Saint-Vougay, protected by its imposing walls with square towers at the corners. Right: the Notre-Dame chapel of Kreisker in Saint-Pol-de-Léon, crowned by its magnificent bell tower, 77 meters high.

CHATEAU DE KERJEAN

Ensconced in the high forests in the midst of the rich market gardening plain of Léon, the Château of Kerjean is enclosed in a vast square circuit of walls protected by its moat. Some call the most sumptuous mansion in Léon the "sleeping beauty". Louis Barbier, nephew of Hamon, canon of Léon, built it in the new style around 1580, welcoming the Renaissance here with reminiscences of Anet, the château of Diane de Poitiers, the lady of the crescent moon. Kerjean is Renaissance: sundry churches in the Valée de l'Elorn were inspired by its lesson. A magnificent well with a cupola supported on Corinthian columns highlights the interior court flanked by annexes. The main body is set at the back, although the wing containing the hall of honor was destroyed by fire. The dormer windows, the chimney stacks, the mansard roofs, together with the fine lanterns in the foreground form an ideal type of château which has been called the Versailles of Brittany and which has now begun to come out of its lethargy.

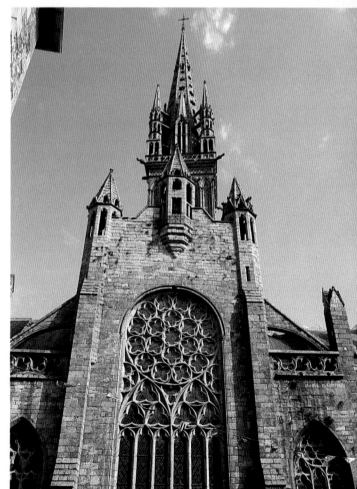

ROSCOFF

Life in Roscoff beat to the rhythm of its successive harbors: the ancient *Rosko-goz*, of which practically nothing remains; the *rade du Vil*, occupied by pleasure boats; the *port of the caseyeurs and the Johnnies* who left to sell their onions door to door to the English housewives and, after 1974, the *deepwater port* at Pointe de Bloscon with its lines to Ireland and Great Britain. The white **Chapel of Sainte-Barbe**, venerated by the sailors, is tutelary guardian of the site. In the town, the 16th-century houses with their fine dormer windows offer the best of their wine cellars out on the sidewalks. Deposits of wealthy merchants are decorated with chimneys marked with strange abbreviations engraved by ship owners of long ago.

A strange enticing city, Roscoff is poetry. It was here that Tristan Corbière composed the couplets of his "Amours jaunes", that Littré recovered from the fatigues of his Dictionnaire de la langue française. Louis-Ferdinand Céline wrote his thesis on medicine at the Biological Station of Lacaze-Duthiers. A marine spa, the natural iodine in the immense estran de Roscoff alternates with the skill of a highly qualified medicinal art.

The **church of Notre-Dame de Kroaz-Baz** was built in the 16th century by parishioners weary of the yoke of the neighboring Saint-Pol. The belfry and the elegant lanterns rise up on the bell tower. Caravels sail along the walls, carved with all sails hoisted. A large retable with twisted columns stands in the sanctuary, while the side aisles house an altarpiece with the apostles, an altarpiece of the Virgin, and one in alabaster from Nottingham. It must be added that the strange name of Notre-Dame de Kroaz-Baz comes from the cross which stands at the embarcadero for the nearby *Ile de Batz* with its incomparable, mild climate.

Facing page: two views of the harbor of Roscoff.

Roscoff, the church of Notre-Dame de Croaz-Baz. The name derives from the fact that it lies a few steps from the cross which marks the old landing stage for the Ile de Batz.

THE PARISH CLOSE

In the area of the feudal countship of Léon this original formula for the organization of the space around the church became a form of art in the 17th century as a result of an extremely favorable historical and economic context. It was also to be found in Bretagne, above all Lower Brittany where it became a supplementary element of a cultural identity that was already distinguished by the Breton tongue. The quality of the soil and the mildness of the climate favored the growing of linen in the area of Léon, and therefore a cottage industry of weaving and the exportation of cloth via sea as early as the 15th century. The wealth that resulted from these activities contributed to the development of the parishes in the 17th century. They capitalized these benefices, managed the communal goods efficiently and ceaselessly invested in the parish close, which became the visible symbol of the village community. Indeed, patronage was no longer in the hands of the lords, but in that of the lay parish assembly, a social body dominated by the emergence of new notables. From the end of the 16th to the 18th centuries they were quick to accept the dictates of the Renaissance, Baroque and Classic styles. The wealth at their disposal led to a continuous patronage of the arts in all fields. As the population increased, the Gothic structure of the church was successively enlarged and the imposing bell towers were erected. The administrators of the parish saw to the construction of the south porch under which the council met after mass: local cults and catholic devotion were expressed in the multiplication of the retables and the statues; and the parish feasts were the occasion for a display of ornaments, liturgic goldwork, gleaming banners. One can understand why, in this context, competition developed between the parishes which resulted in local rivalries. Examples are to be found in the buildings nearby: the Beaumanoir chevet of Saint-Melaine in Morlaix, dating to the 15th century, was imitated in Bodilis and in the ossuary of Saint-Thégonnec; the Gothic Kreisker spire of Saint-Pol-de-Léon is found in Lampaul-Guimiliau and in Bodilis; the Renaissance work of the château of Kerjean, of the 1580s, finds its echo in the portal of the close of Saint-Thégonnec and in the apostle porches of Bodilis, Tremaouezan and Landerneau. Later the models become more national, such as the domes of the bell towers of Pleyben and of Saint-Thégonnec. To be kept in mind also is the fact that the patrons had at their disposal highly competent building masters and sculptors of national and international culture, formed in the ateliers of the royal Navy in Brest.

Lampaul-Guimiliau, ensemble built between 1533 and 1680. The steeple was struck down in 1809.

Bodilis, the bell tower (1570) and the porch (1601). As at Lampaul-Guimiliau, the bell tower is modelled on that of Kreisker in Saint-Pol-de-Léon.

Lampaul-Guimiliau. Above: glory beam. Right: tabernacle.

LAMPAUL-GUIMILIAU

In Lampaul-Guimiliau, the relatively low building is aglow with its splendid polychrome woodwork. The *poutre de gloire* (glory beam) of the late 16th century supports a 17th-century Crucifixion and presents the scenes of the Passion and the twelve sibyls in a picturesque style where the rather naive use of lively colors reveals local craftsmanship. On the other hand the artistic quality of the tabernacle, the splendid side altars, the fonts and the organ tribune, all of the 17th century, is undeniable. Imitations of Northern painters such as Rubens are evident in certain panels of the altarpiece. Two works testify to the intervention of foreign artists: the *Passion altarpiece* of the 16th century, which was imported from Antwerp, and the *Entombment* executed in 1676 by Chavagnac, native to Auvergne, who held the position of master sculptor in the port of Brest.

Guimiliau, south facades and parish close.

Facing page: the Calvary of Guimiliau, executed between 1581 and 1588. In the upper tier the Baptism of Christ, procession with the Carrying of the Cross, Descent into Limbo. Below: Visitation, Washing of the Feet, Annunciation.

GUIMILIAU

Architecturally the landscape of Guimiliau is a fine example of how these ensembles were formed between the early 16th and the late 17th centuries. On the left, the bell tower-porch with its turret leads to the belfry; then a vast chapel in which an extraordinary baldaquin is set over the baptismal font, and with an adjacent ossuary of around 1630. In the center, the great portal laden with ornaments and sculpture was built between 1606 and 1617. The facade is extended in a series of gables which correspond to the side chapels: on the right a vast quadrilobate sacristy, erected in 1683; at the east end, a second ossuary of 1648 in the form of an autonomous chapel which also contains a retable. The play of masses in this ensemble is exceedingly varied and bristling with spires, an elaborate backdrop for the large late 16th-century *Calvary*. In contrast to the pyramidal Calvaries of, for instance, Saint-Thégonnec, this one consists of a large square body on which 27 scenes unfold without any apparent logic. Actually there seems to be an underlying theological theme. The calvary is as much a work of art as it is a permanent means for religious preaching and teaching. In their extraordinarily picturesque details and naive execution the sculptures are brimming with life. Lastly, the monumental portal, closed by an iron gate, leads to the close, while side passages, with flagstones prevent animals from entering. From baptism to the funeral rites, the entire apparatus required by the religious life of a Christian is included in this impressive order and with a sumptuousness that strikes the imagination.

The organization of the parish close obeys pre-Christian traditions. The idea of a closed space set aside for specific purposes is essential. Around the buildings lies not a cemetery but a transitional zone halfway between the profane and the religious. The ossuary and the south porch can be considered liturgical and symbolic stages in the approach to the universe of the sacred, be it the services or that of the afterworld.

Facing page. Above: south facades and parish close of Saint-Thégonnec. Below: Calvary of 1610, with offering table. The crucifix is flanked by two knights, the Virgin and Child is flanked by St. Peter and St. Paul. The thieves bound to the cross wear contemporary breeches.

Interior of the choir of Saint-Thégonnec: wainscotting of 1730, pulpit of 1683, and side reredos of the 17th century.

SAINT-THEGONNEC

The wealthy notables and parishioners of Saint-Thégonnec carried this desire for ostentation to its extreme in continuing their construction campaigns from 1573 to 1730 and in making their close, the last one to be erected in Léon, particularly monumental. Without abandoning the structure of the Gothic chevet, the master carvers went overboard in loading the ossuary chapel, as well as the triumphal portal, with an elaborate Renaissance decoration. In contrast to this amassing of ornamentation, the tower, which is contemporary with that of Pleyben, is an imposing mass, crowned by lanterns. The nave and the chevet, rebuilt at the turn of the 18th century, are monumental in form, but neutral, enclosing a well-lit unobtrusive space, in which the important woodwork comes into its own. The numerous retables and the pulpit suffice to make the liturgical space highly theatrical. The pulpit provides the transept walls with a focal point,

presenting statues and groups of sculpture framed by an elaborate ornamentation.

They are the work of local artists, architects from Morlaix and Lampaul, sculptors from Morlaix, Landivisiau and Brest, all employed as decorators on the king's fleet under construction in Brest. The esthetic choices of the artists and the tastes of the patrons eloquently comment on the Catholic religion as the Counter-Reformation wished: theological in its principles, but extremely visual in its manifestations and appealing to the heart and the fantasy, touched by the beauty of the works of art as if they were a reflection of divine grace. Works of art fell into the category of good works realized by the village as a whole thanks to its wealth and which were a stage in the achievement of community welfare. Here, as in other closes, inscriptions, written in Breton, French, or Latin, and often inscribed on the facades of the ossuary, invite reflection not so much on death itself as on the frailty of the social position and the brevity of life, as in Ploudery and La Martyre.

SIZUN

In the 17th centuries the parishes (between Léon and Cornouaille) which border on the Monts d'Arrée, now the regional Parc d'Armorique, enjoyed the same economic prosperity as did the rich linen parishes of Léon, Sizun to the north of the old mountain massif, or Pleyben to the south. The architecture attests to the activities of the linen industry, carried out in country houses with their characteristic gables at the back of the court and a covered external staircase. But here too the most tangible sign is the development of the parish close. As in Léon, the architectural adventure began at the end of the 16th century and was expressed in Renaissance forms. At the time, elaborate religious fetes attracted considerable crowds, and the preacher could address the assembly from the top of the platform of the majestic portal of Sizun, which resembles a real arch of triumph. As for the ossuary, it still serves as charnel house as well as mortuary chapel: its size is a sign of the importance this society accorded death. Inside the church of Sizun the artists, who came from the maritime ateliers, have, in the course of the 17th century, completely filled the space with a series of sumptuous furnishings. Particularly notable is the ability, elaborate but sober, of the 18th-century masters; in Sizun they brilliantly succeeded in adapting the Gothic form of the 15th-century bell tower of Léon, where the feeling for verticality marks the parish landscape.

Two views of the parish close of Sizun: triumphal gate, ossuary of the 1590s and bell tower of 1728.

Above: La Martyre. Deposition from the Cross in kersanton granite, 16th century. Right: Pleyben, first Gothic bell tower, tower of 1588 and calvary of 1555.

LA MARTYRE

The beginnings of the parish close of La Martyre, one of the earliest, on the boundary between Léon and Cornouaille, along the valley of the Elorn, date to the middle of the 15th century. This place of pilgrimage, famous for its horse fair, was the particular concern of the duc de Bretagne: the numerous coats of arms on the Gothic porch make it a true lesson in feudal history.

PLEYBEN

At Pleyben the master builders grafted a lovely sacristy onto the nave of the church. Its central plan is pure Renaissance and, 130 years later, the architects succeeded in maintaining the unity of the ensemble when the domes they built for the sacristy recalled those of the bell tower and its late 16th-century lanterns. This solicitude for continuity is also illustrated at Pleyben in the complementery structures added to the great Calvary by the atelier of Ozanne, a family of architects, engravers, draftsmen and painters who worked for the king in Brest.

LA ROCHE-MAURICE

La Roche-Maurice is a good example of a type of church frequently encountered: a long sloping roof carried on low walls that look as if they were rooted to the ground, and a gabled facade into which the bell tower-porch with overhanging galleries is inserted. The remarkably homogeneous ensemble was erected between 1539 and 1640. On the fine ossuary, the *Ankou*, a representation of death armed with a javelin, leads the dance of death in the midst of inscriptions. Renaissance decor, consisting of the large stained-glass window and the rood screen, illuminate the interior and lend the necessary animation to the simple rather weighty space. Typical of the Breton church is the still medieval love of color and warm tones. In the *stained glass*, the work of an atelier from Quimperois, scenes from the Passion flank the large Crucifixion scene in the center; at the top are the coats of arms of the Rohan, the local lords and owners of the neighboring castle-fort. The same crowding of figures and ornamental details appears in the *rood screen* of the middle of the 16th century. While the execution of the figures is rather mediochre, the ornamental Renaissance sculpture, which includes a few Gothic monsters and leaves, is of high quality.

Left: bell tower of 1589 and ossuary of 1639. Below: rood screen of the 16th century.

Facing page: Renaissance decor. Above: stained glass window with the Passion, 1539. Below: figures of the Apostles on the rood screen.

LE FOLGOET

In the midst of the rich lands of Léon, ever since the Middle Ages the basilica of Le Folgoët has been one of the leading pilgrimage sites in Brittany, with an affluence in September of thousands of the faithful to worship the miraculous statue of Our Lady. Between 1422 and 1460 the construction was sustained by the Duc de Bretagne, whose statue is here, and by other important personages, which explains the quality of the architecture and the sculpture, above all for the *apostle porch* and the *rood screen*, both in kersanton granite. This volcanic stone, quarried in the Rade de Brest, permits the detail typical of Flamboyant Gothic. The rood loft is unique and outstanding, its lines forming an elegant somber openwork screen set between the nave and the choir, inundated with light by the tall window. More than other famous pilgrimage sites, le Folgoët is the historical expression of the Marian devotion and the artistic projects it inspired.

Facing page: Roch'h Trévézel in the Monts d'Arrée, massif of the primary era, cross-grained with hard schist, and overlooking a swampy peat bog. A moor of gorse and heath covers these inspiring surroundings.

Right: south facade, calvary and commemorative monument of the 19th century in Folgoët. Below: two works in kersanton granite inside the church: a 16th-century devotional figure and the 15th-century rood screen.

Following pages. Left: oyster beds at low tide and clam farming at Landéda; right: the lighthouse of the Ile Vierge at Lilia in Plouguerneau, the tallest lighthouse in France (77 m.), lighted in 1902.

63

LES ABERS

In *Pays des Abers* (Wrac'h Benoit, Ildut) the wealth comes from the sea which penetrates deeply into the low plateau, cutting into the hostile banks. Algae and oysters, crustaceans and mussels are intensively exploited, using modern methods of gathering and management. Danger also comes from the sea with the violent currents and the reefs, which jut out from the spits or bar the bays. To safeguard the mariners, over the centuries signal stations and, later, lighthouses were built on the isles, such as the **Ile Vierge**, or on the spits, such as **Kermorvan** or **Saint-Mathieu**.

The force of the sea, the blankets of froth which cover the rocks during storms, often make the precautions taken by man vain. No one can forget the time the Super Tanker (Amoco Cadiz) ran aground on the *Pointe de Portsall* in the spring of 1978 and of the "black sea" which polluted the beaches and the mudflats.

Enemy fleets also came from the sea, raiding and pillaging. The coast itself is scattered with solid defenses. From the batteries of the 17th century to the blockhaus of the Atlantic Wall (1943), they are reminders that throughout the centuries England was the enemy. The dangers of the sea and the risks of invasion have nourished stubborn myths. This is why the Pays des Abers is called the "coast of legends".

Behind this everchanging world lies the *plateau of Léon*, cut by short sunken valleys. A land of farmers where the presence of cultivated fields has not succeeded in erasing the melancholy mood of the windswept land and where truck farms are interspersed with chapels and healing fountains. In a word, these woods and pastures dotted in all directions by hamlets, manor houses, megaliths and cemeteries, remain the land of "Breton mystery".

Facing page: two views of Conquet. Above: the Pointe de Kermorvan and the imposing fortification that protects the small port; below: the ford and the port.

Below: a casayeur at the wharf in Conquet.

OUESSANT

Point of embarkation for the islands is **Conquet**. The English have repeatedly set fire to this small village which was one of the principal centers of cartography in 16th-century Europe. The islands lie low on the horizon and with them a thousand rocks, lighthouses and signal stations, beacons in the currents. The ship skirts *Béniquet*, *Quéménès*, *Trielen*, as well as unsettled lands left to the rabbits and the birds, and it anchors at *Molène* where a handful of faithful islanders cling to this dangerous land. After passing the *Fromveur*, one of the most violent currents in the West, one arrives at **Ouessant**, the "highest island". On the east high cliffs border this rarely seen bascule plateau (8 x 4 km) which remains the watch tower of the West. At each end, a lighthouse: on the West the imposing *Creach'h*, and on the East, the *Stiff*, doubled by a lookout tower where radar installations unceasingly watch over the comings and goings in the English Channel. More than 400 ships each day travel over these highways of the sea.

Facing page: two views of the Ile d'Ouessant, now practically deserted, formerly a wheat field. Above: the lighthouse of Stiff (1615). Below: the windmill of Gouzoul.

Left: the church of Lampaul (1860) and its bell tower, offered by the English after the shipwreck of a steamer in June 1896. Below: the northwest coast of the Ile d'Ouessant.

Plougonvelin, the Pointe de Saint-Mathieu: a signal tower and a lighthouse (1835) overlooking the ruins of a vast abbey (13th cent.).

Facing page. Above: the city and the arsenal of Brest. Below: the fortified gates (15th cent.) of the castle. This is the only opening in the walls and it leads to the Prefecture Maritime.

BREST

The strategic importance of the feudal countship of Léon, its potentialities as roadstead, led to the creation of a town as soon as the royal power decided to establish a military port and an arsenal here. In 1631 Richelieu installed it on the *Penfeld*, a short, narrow, deeply embanked ford. A town soon sprang up on the plateau, protected by the Château, a powerful trapezoid fortress continually reinforced. Three and a half centuries later, the structure, the dragging and the repairing of the war fleet became the principle reason for Brest's existence and the means of livelihood for the 200,000 inhabitants. In the words of J. Michelet: "the power of France is concentrated in the tip of France" (1833).

During World War II the city was bombed more than 150 times on account of its strategic site and the concentration of arms. After its destruction, a new start was made in 1945 and the ramparts, boulevards, passageways and stairs which had previously enchanted visitors and artists were replaced with a flat unimaginative geometric town. The Penfeld still cuts the town in two: to the east *Brest même*, administrative, commercial, the "French" part; to the west, *Recouvrance*, the popular quarter, more "Breton" with its laborers and sailors. A drawbridge (1954) unites the two banks. The **Castle** went practically unscathed through the war and the town's past and present coexist here in the remains of the Roman fort (3rd cent.) and the imposing maritime prefecture. The Admiralty maintains the headquarters of the Atlantic forces here.

The collections of the **Musée de la Marine**, installed in the vast restructured keep, enlarged in the 14th to 18th centuries, magnificently evoke the times of wooden vessels, maneuvers with sails, and the discovery of far-distant lands. The modern fleet lies scattered throughout the 15,000 hectares of the roadstead. The naval school and the *Ile Longue*, submarine pen for the Force Océanique Stratégique, are on the south bank.

In comparison to this immense base, the activities of the commercial port and the reparation of ships, directly hit by the crisis, seem rather modest. Hopes are set on high technology, laying claim to the high seas, and in applied research which takes the *Ifremer* out to exploit the seas. It is clear that the future of Brest, whether civil or military, lies in the sea.

Brest, the Musée de la Marine installed in the dungeon of the castle.

Facing page: the west side of the Calvary of Plougastel (1602-04).

PLOUGASTEL

Long isolated, the peninsula of Plougastel, with its ridges of quartzite and its sunken valleys, its fords and its ports, is one of the most seductive epitomes of the Pointe de Bretagne. It was famous for its strawberries but they have been replaced by prosperous hothouse cultures of vegetables or flowers.

One can venture forth in search of the superb points of view over the roadsteads and the narrows, the town and the port of Brest, to cross the hamlets, to look for the fountains and the chapels. A captivating

Plougastel, the Calvary. Above: Hell, terrifying image meant to divert the faithful from the Devil's Path. *Opposite, above:* Jesus and the Doctors; *below:* Christ before Pilate.

patrimony where the jewel is the monumental **Calvary** that dominates the center of the small market-town. Built as an ex-voto on the site where the plague was brought to a halt in 1598, it was finished in 1604, restored in 1870 and retouched in 1950. It is the latest of the great Breton calvaries, a sublime challenge to time, its 150 figures in stone silently teaching us the story of Christ. The contrasting scenes of this memorial still continue to play an essential role in the sermons of Basse-Bretagne.

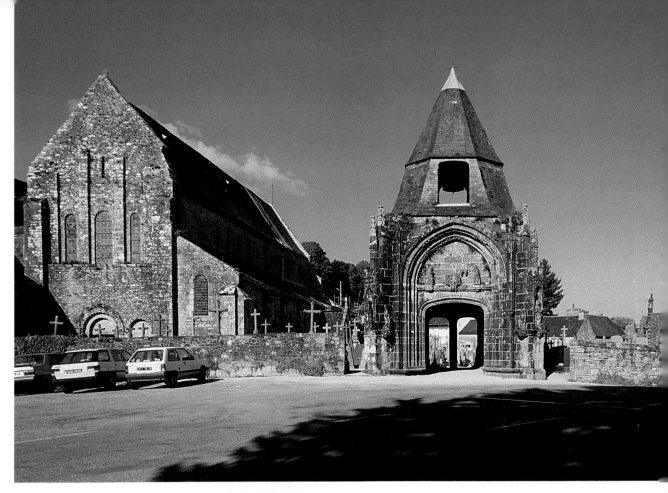

Above: the parish close of Daoulas. From left to right: the Romanesque church, the old porch shifted in 1876, and the Chapel of Sainte-Anne. Left: the cross in the cemetery, in kersanton granite (1590).

DAOULAS

Off the main route, Daoulas is a tranquil village. On the heights, vestiges of a rich Romanesque abbey have been discovered where the church — now the parish church — was thoroughly remodeled in the 19th century. At the time, the remains of the cloister were rebuilt, making the most of the elegant capitals and an exceptional stone basin. The imposing 16th-century porch, a gusty mixture of flamboyant Gothic and Renaissance styles, was then also transferred. Formerly set against the south aisle, it served henceforth as bell tower and entry to the graveyard.

An ossuary (1589) shifted to behind the church in 1876, a cross in kersanton granite, and the ravishing St. Anne Chapel (17th cent.) complete an ensemble which testifies to the relationship the Bretons have maintained for eight centuries with the sacred. The church of *Rumengol* and its Baroque retables should also be seen in the same spirit: sumptuous harmonies between popular mysticism and skilful execution.

Above: the estuary of the Aulne and the slopes of Ménez-
Hom. Right: the sidewalk in Place de l'Eglise in Crozon.

AULNE VALLEY

The Aulne, the main river of Finistère, empties into the
roadstead of Brest through a deep ford. The varied landscapes of the ample meanders towards *Térénez* or *Trégar-
van* and the steep banks to be seen from the belvedere of
Rosnoën are little known. One can make out to the south
the flat ridges of the **Ménez-Hom**, modest hills (330 m.)
which, the first obstacle towards the ocean, take their
charm from the windy mountains above the pines.
A rocky projection bars the estuary, producing a remarkable haven and favoring the microclimate. This is where
Landévennec lies, now apparently only a small village at
the edge of the shore but actually one of the most important sites in Breton history, nay of Christianity, in the
west. At the end of the 5th century Guenole founded the
oldest abbey in Brittany here. Abandoned in the 18th century, destroyed in the Revolution, it was rebuilt on the
slope by the Benedictines (1953-58) and overlooks the
vast extension of Romanesque ruins.

Above: the strand of Véryac'h and the Pointe de la Tavelle, in the bay of Penhir. Left: Pointe de Dinan, known as the ''Château''.

Facing page: the ''Château de Dinan'', detail of the western spit.

CROZON PENINSULA

The Crozon Peninsula stretches out to the west of the Aulne: an immense cross of sandstone and schist, an interminable succession of ridges and valleys, a rich museum of natural science — structural forms, primary fossils, marine erosion, coastal deposits, various birds. . . to the south the *Cap de la Chèvre* half closes the bay of Douarnenez; on the north the *Pointe des Espagnols* reduces the entry to the Rade de Brest to a narrow neck. This will furnish an idea of its strategic value, continuously renewed from prehistoric times to the present era of nuclear defense.

Once farmland, the countryside now stands empty. The sandy moors and the fallow lands have taken over the fields; the villages, huddled together or lined up along the road, live mostly on summer tourism. The famous seaside resort of Morgat, the farflung beaches, the pleasure craft, wind surfing, give new life to these varied austere spaces where one gets the feeling, more so here than elsewhere, of having arrived at land's end, the feeling of living face to face with the unknown.

Above: Pointe de Penhir and the monument to the Bretons of Free France (1951). Left: the cliff of Penhir (60 m.).

Facing page: the beach of Penhat and the Pointe du Toulinguet, where the signal tower keeps watch over the entry to Brest.

CAMARET

All the way to the west, Camaret is the jewel of the peninsula. Its safe bay was for a long time the outer harbor of Brest. A long natural breakwater protects the port; a chapel (1527) and a tower built by Vauban add to its picturesqueness. It has attracted painters for the last 150 years. Unfortunately, the wealth brought not long ago by lobster fishing has vanished and depression has set in everywhere.

The void of the surface of the sea, the solitude of the moors and beaches, the grandeur of the ragged spits make this cape a space outside of time, an imposing refuge which seduces artists and writers. It should be noted that all the great sites of the Crozon Peninsula — from the rounded mass of the *Ménez-Hom* up to the sharp cliffs of **Penhir** — consist of the same hard rock: the Armorican sandstone. The slope of the strata, now horizontal, now vertical, conditions the forms and infinitely varies the spectacular effects of this wild and enduring landscape. Military interests have long protected these places from anarchical building speculation, preserving them in their captivating aspect of Genesis.

SAINTE-ANNE-LA-PALUD

In the Middle Ages the bishopric of Quimper comprised the southern half of Finistère and a part of Morbihan and the Côtes du Nord. The legend of the town of Ys, swallowed up by the bay of Douarnenez, testifies to the mythical origins of Cornouaille: thanks to the intervention of a saint, king Gradlon was able to flee on horseback the wave unloosed through the fault of his daughter Dahub; he is depicted at the top of the gable of the cathedral of Quimper. On the shores of this bay on the last Sunday in August the most important *Pardon* in Cornouaille is enacted here in Sainte-Anne-la-Palud with a great affluence of pilgrims. Each parish is represented by a group in their Sunday best and by symbolical objects: heavy silver crosses made in the 16th and 17th centuries by Breton goldsmiths; small statues carried around on stretchers, as if the Virgin of that parish had come to pay a visit to her mother; lastly sumptuous banners, with rich passementeries and embroideries, with inscriptions in Breton. The Pardon is also the occasion to exhibit the traditional costumes decorated with floral or geometric embroidery, characteristic of Breton folk art. There is a great diversity of lace coifs and openwork or pleated collars. These costumes, which identify each town, originated and were developed in the course of the 19th century, notably the famous cap in the form of a sugar loaf which continues to get taller.

Two pictures of the procession of the pardon of Sainte-Anne-la-Palud.

Facing page: coifs, costumes and collective fervor during the procession.

Above: church and chapel of the Pénity on the Place de Locronan.
Left: group of the Lamentation (around 1550) in the church.

Facing page. Above: a craftsman at work perpetuating the tradition of the "imagiers", sculptors and painters of the past. Below: the lovely Place de Locronan, with its granite houses and its old wells.

LOCRONAN

Another of these religious manifestations, whose roots go deep down in pre-Christian strata, is the *Troménie* of Locronan. The saint venerated in this tiny village is St. Ronan, a hermit bishop of Irish origin who is said to have lived in the 10th century. Popular worship centered on the saint's tomb, in the Pénity, and in the 15th century the interests of the dukes helped construct the Gothic church which was inspired by the cathedral of Quimper. The interior contains important furnishings in wood, made by local artists, such as the *Entombment*, in polychrome wood, with skilfully executed ornaments yet rather awkward in its composition. It is set on the fragments of an altar in kersanton granite dating to the early 16th century. But its cloth industry was what made Locronan famous throughout Europe in the late Middle Ages, attested to by the fine 17th and 18th-century mansions of the weavers and the merchants who ensured the maritime commerce of the cloth which was also produced in the surrounding countryside.

Facing page: the lighthouse of the Vieille, at the extreme point of the continent, keeps watch in the midst of the terrible currents of the Raz de Sein.

On the cliffs of the Pointe du Van, the Chapel of Saint-They and, in the distance, the Baie des Trépassés.

CAP SIZUN

The **Pointe du Raz** and its grand milieu are what one might ideally expect to find at land's end — at the western terminal of the European continent. Everything concurs to impress the visitor who proceeds along the north side of Cap Sizun: the wild reserve for sea birds, the jagged cliffs at the **Pointe du Van** and the solitude of the 17th-century *Chapelle Saint-They*, with its roof tied to the soil in front of the ocean, the name itself of the **Baie des Trépassés** (Bay of the Departed) calling to mind the frequent shipwrecks along the coast, and the romantic site of the Pointe du Raz that continues, in the suspended points of the *lighthouse of the Vieille*, the *Ile de Sein*, and, at the far end of a line of rocks, the *lighthouse of Ar Men* erected in 1881. All this part of Cornouaille consists of a striking succession of extremely varied, arresting landscapes. Set further inland, the farmhouses built in granite ashlar and dating to between the 17th and 19th centuries, are architecturally quite fine.

The south part of Cap Sizun is less austere. It harbors the small city of **Pont-Croix** in a picturesque site on the shores of a stream. The *church of Notre-Dame de Roscudin* is set in the midst of old houses, dating mostly to the 17th century.

The nave, built in the 13th century and revealing English influence, served as a model for numerous religious buildings in Cournouaille. Near the busy port of Audierne, the **Saint-Tugen chapel** in Primelin is a superb Gothic structure of the 16th century which has preserved its important woodwork furnishings, including panel paintings of the 17th century.

Further south, the **chapel of Tronoën** was built in the 15th century. Its large *Calvary*, with a wide plinth with bas-reliefs, is one of the first examples of this type in Brittany. The weathering of the granite in the sea air and the isolated site in the midst of the bare dunes lend it an extraordinary charm.

Above: signal tower and lighthouse of Eckmühl in the Penmarch peninsula. Left; chapel and calvary of Tronoën.

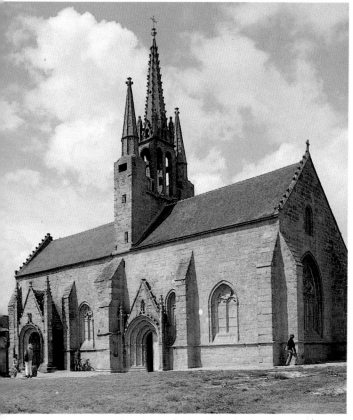

THE PENMARCH PENINSULA

On the other hand, as seen in the museums, the low flat territory of the Penmarch Peninsula was inhabited from prehistoric times. The various towns here played a leading role in Breton economy in the 15th and 16th centuries, in part because of their fisheries and fish-drying installations, but above all because of the international trade practiced by the ship captains who transported merchandise along the entire Atlantic coast, from Portugal to the ports of England and the mouths of the Escaut. The **church of Saint-Nonna** testifies to their activity in the depictions of caravels and fish carved on the porches at the beginning of the 16th century. The granite **lighthouse of Eckmühl** (Phare d'Eckmül), 1897, stands on the Pointe de Penmarch.

THE ODET VALLEY

Between Quimper and the port of Bénaudet, the Odet Valley, 16 km. long, lies along a sinuous route known as Vire-Court, which forms a natural defense as well as a series of outstanding sites which can best be explored by boat. The shores are dotted with castles in vast parks that slope softly or fall off sharply towards the river, with a marvelous array of plants that thrive in this mild climate — rhododendrons, palms, magnolias. The **château of Kerembleiz** was rebuilt in the 19th century in a rather dry neo-Gothic style, with vast out-buildings and auxiliary structures of an English type. **The château of Pérennou** stands on the site of a Roman villa with baths, over which a medieval manor was later built. During the 14th century a warrior-poet who had fought in Italy lived here, and as chance would have it this dwelling was always chosen by scholars and writers. In the 19th century it was rebuilt as a large mansion in an imaginative combination of Medieval and Renaissance styles. At this time the park was transformed into an exuberant romantic garden, full of exotic plants.

Near Quimper, the **château of Lanniron**, an old 15th-century manor, became the bishop's residence. Two country chapels still stand on this bank, the 17th-century **Notre-Dame du Vrai Secours**, and the 16th-century **Saint-Cadou**, characteristic for Cornouaille with its apparatus used in the Pardon — oratory, terrace surrounded by old trees, holy font, from which one can descend towards a silent cove. Further on, at Gouesnach, the small **château de Lanhuron**, built in the 18th century by a councilor to the king, recalls the country houses around Saint-Malo. The entire countryside, traversed by winding shady roads, has that air of intimacy that makes one forget the hustle and bustle of the city.

On the banks of the Odet, the châteaux of Kerembleiz and of Pérennou.

Quimper seen from Mont Frugy.

Facing page. Above: the medieval ramparts flanking the Odet and the bishop's garden. Below: stained-glass window in the cathedral depicting the bishop offering the model of the spires built in 1854 to the Virgin and Saint Corentin.

QUIMPER

Quimper, an ancient town, first Celtic, then Gallo-Roman, was given by King Gradlon to the bishop St. Corentin. As seat of the bishop-count of Cornouaille, in the Middle Ages it became a rich urban center surrounded by ramparts. The **cathedral** rises up above the town which lies in a shallow basin at the back of the Odet estuary. Conceived along the lines of the cathedrals of the Ile-de-France, the addition of various Anglo-Norman features turned this majestic original building into the largest Gothic structure in Brittany. Begun in the 13th century, the great construction yard was not in full swing until around 1500 and finally closed in the 19th century with the erection of the spires in striking homogeneity with the rest of the work. The influence exerted by this monu-ment, with the towers characterized by their long openings, is visible in numerous buildings in Cornouaille. The south portal is a remarkable example of sculpture in the period of the dukes (15th cent.). The vast nave, with its 15th and 16th-century stained glass, is not on an axis with the choir on account of the nature of the terrain and the urban site. In front of the cathedral, the network of sloping streets and alleys still contains a goodly number of old houses. In the *Rue du Guéodet* the corbels on a late 16th-century facade are sculptured with grimacing heads which probably depict the legendary ribalds of the time. The *Rue du Sallé* has one of the loveliest houses, but it is above all the *Rue Kéréon*, the street of the cobblers in the Breton tongue, which still furnishes an idea of what

a medieval street with its overhanging houses was like. One of these has a gable completely covered in slate so as to protect the half-timbering from the weather. On the corner of the *Rue des Boucheries*, a Virgin dated 1552 watches over trading activities which animated the ville close (inner town) of the bishop. Further on is the *Place de la Terre-au-Duc*, lined with old houses, which was under the jurisdiction of the duke and which prolonged the ancient nucleus into a suburb. In the 17th century, austere monumental facades in granite, such as the **Jesuit college**, now a public high school, went up. But it was particularly in the 18th century that merchants and notables began to have fine granite mansions built for themselves, of a type which was then widely used. In the 19th century the urbanization of the piers made it possible to open the town and to connect it, along Mont Frugy, with the *suburb of Locmaria*, where a fine 12th-century Romanesque church stands alongside its 17th-century priory on the banks of the Odet. Architecture of the 19th century, such as the neo-Gothic *prefecture*, the small *theater*, or the lovely bourgeois houses, and that of the 20th century, respected the general scale of the buildings, and thus maintained the undeniable charm of this urban site intact.

Apart from its traditional economy involving above all the food industry, renowned in particular for its canneries and crêpes dentelles, Quimper retains a character both ingenious and true to stock, even in the technological performances of contemporary ventures.

The **Musée Breton** is installed in the former Bishop's Palace, built between the 16th and 18th century, next to the cathedral. The collections are historical, archaeological and ethnographical. The furniture and the costumes on exhibit give a clear picture of the different aspects of the folk art. Some works, such as the *Trinity with St. Anne* of the early 14th century, skilfully composed and executed, reveal a national and even an international style. Other works such as the *Virgin of Pitié* of the 16th century may not be of the same caliber but are still extremely expressive in their very awkwardness, often accentuated by polychrome painting. The same holds true for the furniture with its geometrical ornamentation and even the costumes. The **Musée des Beaux-Arts**, on the other side of the cathedral, is one of the richest in Brittany. It has a superb collection of Flemish and Dutch paintings of the 16th and 17th centuries, as well as a collection of European works of the 18th century. But Brittany itself is also celebrated in the works of the 19th-century painters, numerous and still too little known, and in the paintings of the *school of Pont-Aven* and the *Nabis*. Lastly a room is dedicated to keepsakes of the poet from Quimper, Max Jacob.

Two works preserved in the Musée Breton. Above: Saint Anne, the Virgin and Child. *Below:* Pietà.

Musée des Beaux-Arts. Above: Descent from the Cross *by Pieter Van Mol (17th cent.) from a convent in Saint-Pol-de-Léon. Right:* Breton Studies, *by Emile Bernard, one of the founders of the Pont-Aven school in 1886.*

Craftsmen at work in the faience factory H. B. Henriot in Locmaria and an example of finished work.

Pottery was already being produced in the *district of Locmaria* in antiquity, and the development of faience began around 1700 with the imitation of models from Rouen. Subsequently ceramics became a true creative art, all the more authentic when it was endowed with life by the Breton decorators in figurines, above all of the Virgin, plates in 18th-century taste, highly decorated objects which incorporated elements of folk art, or else, beginning in the 1930s, popular subjects, groups or personages treated with simplicity, in an attempt to catch the initial vivacity in the finished work, painted with brilliant colors enhanced by a geometric decor.

In the museum in Locmaria it is striking to note how, in recent times, the faience factories of Quimper have succeeded in creating a style that can be identified as Breton with works of real decorative quality.

Fine chapels to be found in the environs of Quimper include **Kerfeunten** with stained glass of the early 16th century and **Kerdevot**, in Ergué-Gabéric, a 15th-century building in the country-side of Cornouaille.

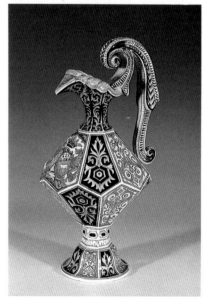

*Examples of faience work
from the manufactories in Quimper.*

QUILINEN

The chapel of Quilinen in the surroundings of Quimper has an unusual 16th-century **Calvary**. Unlike the large compositions on a rectangular plan, loaded with reliefs, as at Tronoën, this Calvary is composed of two overlapping triangles from which the figures range up in tiers in an ascensional movement towards the crucified Christ, shown on the back as the Risen Christ.

CAST

In front of the church of Cast, a sculptural group depicts the *Encounter of St. Hubert with the divine stag*. It was executed around 1540 in the black stone that is peculiar to the Rade de Brest, kersanton granite, which lends great delicacy of execution to the plastic rendering. The scene, unique in Brittany, is spectacular for its intensity. These two works in Quilinen and Cast testify to the skill of the Breton artists. The former, with its sense of architectural composition, succeeds in renewing the formula of the isolated Calvary and represents, as it were, the spiritual function of these small monuments. The latter, in a difficult material, furnishes an extraordinary lesson in the technique and art of sculpture.

Facing page. Above: modern market building, Halles Saint-François. Below: 18th-century dwellings in front of the cathedral.

Right: calvary of Notre-Dame de Quilinen. Below: the Hunt of St. Hubert, in Cast.

Facing page: two views of Bénodet where the estuary of the Odet flows in, the stream that is ''even sweeter than its name'' (G. Apollinaire).

Concarneau, the inner harbor and the ville close.

BÉNODET

''Odet is the bluest and the clearest stream'' sang Guillaume Apollinaire in his *Guetteur mélancolique*.
A mild, sunny climate, the lure of woods and valleys, celebrated by painters, an expanse of water bordered by the Glenan archipelago: each of these reasons by itself suffices to explain the growth of tourism in this part of Cornouaille. The Odet ''the loveliest stream in France'', the land of the ''best cider in the world'', in the ''homeland of pretty women'' (Flaubert), what more is one to ask? The older resorts of **Bénodet**, **Begmeil**, and the more recent ones of **Forêt-Fouesnant** or **Port-la-Forêt** mark the stages in the taking over of a coastline that is fragile and therefore threatened.
After the precocious launching (1950) of the nautical center of Glenan, numerous bases today make this region one of the principal centers for sailing along the entire French coast.

CONCARNEAU

The town of Concarneau originated in a cove, where an island assured its isolation and safety, and soon became a stronghold which the end of the Middle Ages transformed into a stake in the Franco-English conflict. Rebuilt in the second half of the 16th century, the **enceinte** was modified a century later ''in the style of Vauban''. In a period (1670-1810) when, opposite England, Brittany was bristling with fortifications, the **ville close** (inner town) installed artillery platforms and erected the towers which kept watch over the ''porte du passage'' that led to the docks.
But at the end of the Middle Ages the *ville close* (actually a single long street) already had to move outside the walls, into the more exposed suburbs whose status changed when fishing rather than war became the town's principal activity. At present a tourist site, the ville close offers its visitors these two symbols of its past: the re-

Above: the entrance to the ville close. Left: the fish auction.

Facing page: fishing flotilla in Concarneau, third port in France for fresh fish.

stored ramparts and the fishing museum.

Fishing: a centuries-old employment that experienced various changes. In past centuries the "big business" of the town was the sardine. In the 20th century adieu the "blue fillets"! Concarneau then became famous as a tunny port. More than 1600 tunny fishing vessels were active here in 1939.

Today number one in tunny for Europe, Concarneau has enlarged its horizons to the tropical waters of the Gulf of Guinea and the Indian Ocean, which its ships hardly leave at all. The crews fly in every six weeks in waves. Their catch is transformed on the spot and the finished products are transported to Concarneau. More than tropical tunny fishing, the port is now animated by coastal and deep water fishing. Nowadays Concarneau is the third French port for fresh fish and, including the frozen tropical tunny, the first port in France for tonnage and income.

Facing page: various types of Breton costume. Cornouaille alone vaunts about fifteen different kinds of coifs and embroideries.

Above: the folk festival of the filets bleus in Concarneau (the last Sunday in August but one). Left: the "Giz-Fouenn", or fashion of Fouesnant-Rosporden.

The fête des filets bleus

At the beginning of the century, the festival of the blue fillets was created as a means of coming in aid to needy families, hard hit by the sardine crisis of 1902. Nowadays its meaning has changed: it is the showcase for the Breton costume of Cornouaille, in particular the "Giz-Fouenn", the fashion in apparel of Fouesnant-Rosporden, celebrated for its ribboned coif and starched collar, with its complicated architecture. The other styles of Cornouaille are also present, such as the mitre coif and the peacock feather embroideries of the "Bigoudens".

In the variety of its apparel, Cornouaille alone well illustrates the history — actually rather brief — of Breton costume. It made its appearance at the end of the 18th century, and underwent a phase of geographical and social differentiation in the 19th century, with an evolution which led, for the coifs, to an exaggerated emphasis at the beginning of the 20th century, when the mitres of Bigouden reached a height of more than 30 centimeters. But let the visitor beware: Brittany is not only the "Breton" costume. . .

Pont-Aven, the Xavier Grall promenade on the Aven river.

Facing page, above: the temporary exhibition gallery of the Musée de Pont-Aven. Below: the chapel of Trémalo and the statue that inspired Gauguin for his "Christ jaune".

PONT-AVEN

In the 19th century Brittany was extremely popular with artists who were particularly struck by the charm of Pont-Aven, a small village on the side of a hill. As the Aven flows through the town, its capricious waters gush over the granite rocks, are swallowed up by the mill wheels and end their course in the embrace of the sea with its rhythmic tides and animated small port.

Stimulated by new ideas, the artists discovered a nature of infinitely varied colors, and a mild climate ideal for variations on the theme. Their reception in the inns was warm and inexpensive. Jullia Guilloux and Jeanne Gloanec, who opened the first pensions, set the example in willingly giving credit.

Haunted by the idea of "somewhere else" and provoked beyond measure by the city, Paul Gauguin sought isolation, the savage and the primitive. His need to escape

Paris and his lack of money brought him in 1886 to Pont-Aven where he boarded in the Auberge Cloanec, remaining alone, hostile to all friendships. Gauguin returned in 1888. His second meeting with the painter Emile Bernard was this time of capital importance. The confrontation of these two beings searching for the same artistic ideal was a catalyzing element, and resulted in the birth of a revolutionary concept: pictorial synthesism.

Soon a group of painters — Serusier, Moret, Filiger, Slewinski, Maufra, etc. — joined them and experimented the theories elaborated by Gauguin and Bernard, spontaneously forming what art historians call the "School of Pont-Aven".

Before sailing definitely for Tahiti in 1895, where he died in 1903, Gauguin returned to Pont-Aven in 1889 and again in 1894.

Above: west facade of Saint-Fiacre-du-Faouët. Left: the rood screen (1480) and the statue of Duc Jean V in prayer.

SAINT-FIACRE-DU-FAOUET

Saint-Fiacre-du-Faouët and Notre-Dame de Kernascléden are two contemporary chapels that resulted from the patronage of great nobles, near the ducal milieu of Jean V Montfort, whose coats of arms are on the vault of Kernascléden and on the chevet of Saint-Fiacre.

The *rood screen* of Saint-Fiacre is dated 1480. Work of an artist from Tregor, Olivier Le Loergan, ennobled by the duke, it is the oldest rood screen still exant in Brittany. Composed of an enclosure surmounted by an overhanging polychrome tribune, it combines figures from the Crucifixion with allegorical scenes.

KERNASCLEDEN

Notre-Dame de Kernascléden received the benefits of the Vicomtes de Rohan. This well-dated building falls into the years 1430-1460. The atelier which worked on the south porch also worked at Saint-Fiacre, which bears the mark of the Boutteville, local lords.

The anonymous artists who painted the 24 scenes created one of the loveliest ensembles of 15th-century French painting. The Infancy of Christ and His Passion depicted on the vaults and in the tympanums, are countered by the dramatic scenes in the transept — the Danse Macabre and Hell. All the anguish of the 15th century, helpless in the face of sudden death, is to be found here in this vision of St. Paul's, to which Dante also referred.

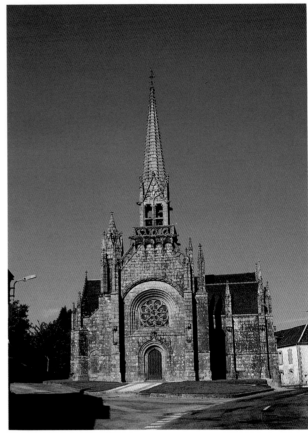

Right: view of the chapel of Notre-Dame de Kernascléden.
Below: paintings in the south arm of the transept. The damned, run through by the branches of a tree, are bitten by the devils who are torturing them with hooks.

Facing page: the alignments of Ménec and Kermario in Carnac: more than 2,000 upright stones.

Carnac: the corridor of dolmens at Kermario.

CARNAC

Megaliths were part of universal cultures. It is however in Brittany, and in particular in the region of Carnac, that the greatest concentration of these "great stones" can be observed.

Set upright, the stones are arranged as an alignment of menhirs: more than 3000 stones give form to the space, from Erdeven to La Trinité-sur-Mer (10 km.), and many have disappeared, victims of time and man. In Carnac, the *Grand Menec* musters together 1099 stones, divided into eleven rows, with an oval enclosure at each end. At **Kermario**, 982 menhirs stand in twelve rows. And there are many others which make Carnac the "museum of megalithism".

Ignoring the medley of fantastic hypotheses, the specialists have interpreted these concentrations as the remains of a great Neolithic religious center, which attract-ed enormous crowds in certain periods of the year (solstice?). The region of Carnac is also that of the dolmens (stone tables), bare frameworks of funerary monuments that were once much more important (*Kermario, Crucuno* in Plouharnel). Enormous tumuli are also to be found here (*Saint-Michel*, Le *Moustoir*), artificial hills about 100 meters long and ten meters high, concealing in their piles of stones burial vaults and coffers, with hearths for cremation.

The **St. Michel tumulus** of Carnac was erected at least 4000 years before Christ and the last dolmens around 2000. These megaliths are the work of Neolithic populations, sedentary farmers and stock-breeders, for whom a knowledge of the rhythm of the seasons was indispensable. They were a folk who identified with the group and who had a strong concept of the afterworld.

QUIBERON

On the map, the Quiberon peninsula, this finger of land fourteen kilometers long pointing towards the open sea, is particularly enticing. It is an ancient rocky island, connected to the continent by a thin line of sand which is no more than a few meters wide at the isthmus of Penthièvre. In 1795 the Republican general Hoche had no trouble in stopping the Royalists who had landed in Carnac here.

Nowadays tourism is everywhere. The slashed cliffs of the *côte sauvage*, the variety of nautical activities, the popularity of thalassotherapy make the Quiberon peninsula, with Carnac and La Trinité-sur-Mer, the high point for tourism in Morbihan, or for that matter in southern Brittany.

Left: the great beach of Quiberon. Below: Port-Maria, but lately one of the first ports for sardines.

BELLE-ILE

In 1886, combing the "needles of Port-Coton", Claude Monet saw the Belle-Ile as a "terrible sinister land, but very beautiful". Any number of other famous names, such as Sarah Bernhardt, have helped make the fame of the largest Breton island. Nevertheless in the beginning it was thought of as a refuge, far from the continent. Subsequently it became a coveted prey, contended by the Spaniards (16th cent.), the English (1761-63), the Germans. A coveted isle, a forbidden isle: the names of Gondi, Fouquet, Vauban and their successors are inseparable from this fortified land, one of the finest examples of military architecture.

Right: the Grotte de l'Apothicairerie in Belle-Ile. Below: the port of Le Palais at the foot of the citadel, an hour from Quiberon by sea.

Facing page, above: the gulf of Morbihan. Below: the "Rivière" d'Auray.

The port of Saint-Goustan, at the back of the "Rivière" d'Auray. Benjamin Franklin landed here on December 6, 1776.

GULF OF MORBIHAN

The Gulf of Morbihan: this admirable body of water, strewn with around thirty islands, spreads out over an area of twenty kilometers between Vannes and the ocean. In 1790 this "small sea" (Mor-bihan) gave its name to this departement for which initially the name of "Côtes du Sud" had been suggested. And indeed the south is present here both in the horizons and in the mildness of the climate. But the gulf, like a coin, has two faces. One is summer, with the crowded beaches and residential shores.

Even the Gallo-Roman Veneti had already built their luxurious villas here, facing the sea, particularly in Arradon. But the "true" gulf can perhaps be discovered in the peace and quiet of late autumn when it is bathed in a soft light that blends the sea, the earth, the sky into watercolor washes, so dear to the artists. These flat, watery horizons offer a great variety of habitats from the broad mudflats, uncovered at low tide, to the grassy zones, salt marshes, the sand and the rocks. All together they make the gulf one of the principle ornithological stations in western Europe. Thousands of barnacle geese come here to winter.

The exploration of the gulf by boat is a must for those who want to discover the vague litoral of the eastern basin, the force of the tidal currents in the western basin, or reach the towns that have sprung up at the back of the estuaries: *Vannes, Auray Saint-Goustan*.

At the mouth of the Rivière d'Auray the menhirs now covered with water, of the *isle of Er-Lannic* near the cairns of *Gavrinis* and of the *Ile-longue* remind us that only a few thousand years ago the level of the ocean was much lower than today. The invasion of the sea, the play of the fractures of the ancient base, all help to make this "morbihan" a living ever-changing realm.

Facade of the cathedral.

Facing page, above: the east frontage of the ramparts of Vannes, opposite the Promenade de la Garenne. Below: the "old" washouses of the early 19th century with, in the background, the Tour du Connétable.

Half-timbered houses in Vannes. Note the stress on corbelling in the older houses.

VANNES

In the Middle Ages Vannes, originally the main Gallo-Roman city of the Veneti, was an episcopal seat and a ducal residence.

The town's fortified **walls** are remarkably well preserved. To the north, the medieval ramparts have replaced the Roman wall which is still visible in places. At the end of the 13th century, the "cloaison" included the lower parts of the town. Vannes became that "city so strong and well provided with gens d'armes", where the French and English troops (commanded by no less a figure than Edward III in person in 1342) clashed during the War of Succession.

The **cathedral** dominates the inner town. It is a building with a single nave, a peculiarity inspired by the southern examples and, it seems, maintained in the 15th century when the Romanesque church was transformed. The dukes encouraged these works, which would make it possible to receive the pilgrims who had flocked to the cathedral since 1419. Vincent Ferrier, a popular Spanish preacher, died in Vannes and was buried there.

Near the cathedral, the **Cohue** (market and seat of jurisdiction), the squares and narrow streets with half-timbered houses perpetuate the atmosphere of the town as it was between 1400 and 1800.

Heritage of almost five centuries of life as a city, the timber facing of Vannes still visible on about 180 houses did not fall victim to the projects which aimed at ripping up the inner city to connect the port with the railroad station (late 19th cent.). The port, which was a source of income for the city, was then in decline. Since it could not accommodate large tonnage ships, Vannes turned its back on the ocean.

Today the principal city of the departement is once more a center of attraction, for tourism has found in the Gulf one of the most favorable conditions for the development of service activities.

Preceded by a column bearing the instruments of the Passion and surmounted by a rooster, the Calvary of Guéhénno stands in the cemetery.

Facing page, above: the town of Josselin, whose origins go back to the Castle on the shores of the Oust. Below: facade of the logis of Jean II de Rohan (early 16th cent.).

CALVARY OF GUEHENNO

In the interior of Morbihan, at the eastern limits of Breton speech, one comes unexpectedly upon the Calvary of Guehenno. This large composition, the only one in Morbihan, dates both to the 16th and to the 19th century. Sculptured in 1550 by F. Guillonic, it is exactly contemporary with the great Breton Calvaries, such as Pleyben or Plougouven. In 1853, it rose from its ruins thanks to the chisels of two deserving parish priests. And now it is no longer easy to distinguish what belongs to each of these two periods, which, three centuries apart, saw its birth and rebirth.

The sculptural narrative here evokes the scenes of the Passion and of Calvary: on a flagstone base the prophets Isaiah, Jeremiah, Ezekiel, and Daniel keep watch. The first platform presents the Entombment for the meditation of the faithful. On the upper platform the Four Evangelists, seated, frame the scene of the Passion: Christ carrying the cross between a soldier and Veronica. Lastly, behind a Pietà, rises the cross of the Savior, as if it were springing from the dream of Jesse. The bas-reliefs

decorating the sides and illustrating scenes of the Last Judgement were carved in 1853.

A composite work of the 16th and 19th centuries, the Calvary of Guehenno testifies to the maintenance of the tradition of the master carvers and, in addition, may also express the persistence of the same forms of piety in the rural world from which it came.

JOSSELIN

A valley in a wooded region, a castle, a fortress church turned basilica: this is Josselin, whose origins date back to the 11th century. The founders, Guéthenoc, lord of Porhoët, and his son Josselin, had at the time settled on pioneer ground. When one of their descendants settled in Rohan in the 12th century, further upstream, the Oust became the axis of the viscounty, with all of 59 parishes in the 15th century, extending from the region of Loudéac to that of Ploërmel. Around the castle, the inner city profitted by the anchorage of Rohan. A merchant town,

Above: the imposing facade of the castle (14th-16th cent.) begun by Olivier de Clisson and remodelled by Jean II de Rohan. Left: the half-timbered houses in the town recall the power of the merchant bourgeois classes under the Ancien Régime.

under the Ancien Régime it was one of the 42 Breton towns to be represented in the Etats de Bretagne.

Of the first castle, without doubt in wood, that of Guéthenoc, nothing remains. It may have been built on the same sheer schist spur where the foundations, now razed, of the 12th century towers are still to be found. Olivier IV of Clisson, high constable of France in 1380 and husband of Marguerite de Rohan, acquired the castle by exchange in the 1370s. He turned it into a fortress. The towers of Josselin can apparently be connected to the Castle of Blain, also a Clisson property.

As seen today, the castle bears the mark of Jean II de Rohan (1452- -1516). He built the great dwelling whose airy facade overhangs, on the side of the river, the fortified curtain walls and the towers, on top of what Olivier de Clisson had done. On the garden side, the monotony which might have resulted from a long alignment of 70 meters is interrupted by the importance given to the upper parts of the building in flamboyant Gothic style, and a balustrade with an ever-changing decor. A sign of the new times: an inner staircase, flight after flight, the oldest known in France.

The castle, abandoned at the time of Richelieu (Henri II

Above: the church of Notre-Dame du Roncier, created thanks to the generosity of important personalities. It was a center for preachinq and is still a pilgrimage site. Right: the pulpit in metal and wrought iron (18th cent.) inside the church.

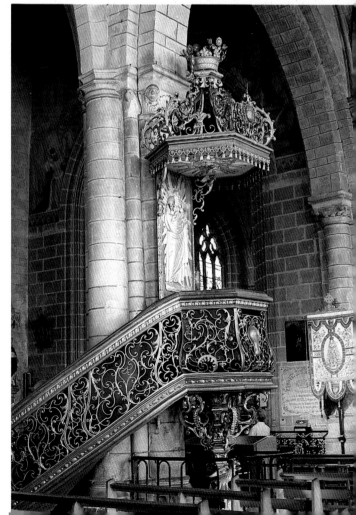

of Rohan was the head of a Calvinistic group), was restored by the Rohan family in the 19th century. Josselin de Rohan, senator of Morbihan and mayor of Josselin, still lives there today.

Notre-Dame du Roncier, the fortress chapel which became a parish church and then a basilica, is a composite work which owes its originality to the generosity of the different benefactors: Olivier de Clisson, the Rohan (before they became connected with the Reformation; then, in the 19th century for the windows), the bishop of Saint-Malo, etc.

The spacious nave dates from the 15th century. It opens into a building which is still a place of pilgrimage (tradition reports the discovery in a thornbush of a miraculous statue of the Virgin) and which was a center for preaching, welcoming Vincent Ferrier in 1418. In the 18th century, it received a pulpit in metal and wrought iron.

In the neighborhood of the basilica (*Rue des Vierges*, *Rue Olivier de Clisson*) the half-timbered houses of the 16th and 17th centuries, decorated with caryatids and sculptured scenes of the Hunt, evoke the power of the merchant and cloth manufacturing bourgeois classes under the Ancien Régime.

The Cours Cambronne and the statue of general Cambronne.

NANTES

Nantes is the birthplace of a duchess, twice queen of France, Anne of Brittany, of an author of adventure novels, Jules Verne, and of a famous crisp cooky, the Petit-Beurrelu — all emblematic figures which could very well go into the making of an allegory. But it would take even longer to tell how a small Gallic port became a powerful ducal city, how a thriving merchant town prospered to become the Atlantic metropolis which Nantes is today.

It is difficult to say precisely when the little town founded by the *Namneti*, from whom it took its name, began. In the heart of Gaul, set at the very end of the estuary of the Loire, Nantes already revealed its double function as river and ocean port in Roman times. When invasion threatened at the beginning of the Middle Ages, the town built a circuit of walls and became the stake in a bitter struggle for influence amongst the Bretons, Francs and Normans until 937 when Alain Barte-Torte (Wrybeard) reconstituted the kingdom of Bretagne and took Nantes. Until the 15th century the city vied with Rennes in establishing its hold over ducal Bretagne and sought to maintain its independence from the kingdom of France.

The accession of Duc Jean V in 1399 was the beginning of a veritable golden century for the city, which reached its zenith with the reign of Anne of Brittany, shortly before François I reunited the duchy and the kingdom. The 15th-century dukes made Nantes the real capital of Brittany. They rebuilt a great castle where they resided, an immense cathedral, and founded a university. The port then played an important role in the maritime trade of the west, which was to grow until the 18th century. In the 16th century, Nantes exported the wines of the Loire valley and the salt of Brittany to northern Europe and her port was essential to the coastal trade between Spain and the Netherlands. With the development of commerce with the colonies at the end of the 17th century, Nantes got her second wind and permitted the merchants and shipping companies to enrich themselves by importing colonial products or by the slave trade.

In the 18th century, this thriving town of the France of the Enlightenment endeavored to change her medieval

General view and detail of the fountain in the Place Royale: the city of Nantes is dependent on the Loire and its affluents.

aspect. The ramparts were torn down and replaced by thoroughfares, new buildings went up, and new quarters transformed Nantes into an active, elegant and "bourgeois" town. In spite of the shock of the Revolution, and of the economic difficulties at the beginning of the 19th century, Nantes maintained an important role in Atlantic trade. When silting up of the Loire reduced the capacities of the port, an auxiliary port was built in *Saint-Nazair* in the 1850s, which permitted larger ships to be accommodated. An intense activity all along the estuary, where the great trading ships (merchant) flank the naval construction yards and the factories, famous for canning and cookies, thus marked the last century. Victim of the tragic air raids of world War II, the project for the reconstruction of the town mirrored the new urban developments of the years 1950 to the present.

In spite of these transformations, Nantes still has its privileged places where history lives on. The curious belfry carillon of the **church of Saint-Croix** rises up in the middle of the old medieval town, with its winding net-

work of narrow streets where a few half-timbered houses of the 15th and 16th centuries can still be found. Close by is the majestic silhouette of the **cathedral Saint-Pierre** which dominates the whole old town and is the work of Duc Jean V. Its total reconstruction, replacing a precedent Romanesque building, was undertaken in 1434 by the architects Guillaume de Danmartin and Mathelin Rodier. The great western facade, finished at the end of the 15th century, has three richly sculptured portals. The construction of the tall nave with side aisles continued to the middle of the 17th century when work on the choir was begun. It was not finished until 1891 and preserves the same architectural structures which made it possible to complete the building in a completely homogeneous style, a perfect example of late Gothic art. In the south arm of the transept, the *tomb of Duc François II*, a spirited example of funerary sculpture of the early 16th century, was created between 1502 and 1507 by the sculptor Michel Colombe. Two reclining figures depict the duke and his second wife, Marguerite de Foix, and four statues, symbolizing the Virtues, guard the tomb.

Left: the west facade of the cathedral of Saint-Pierre. Below: detail of the three portals.

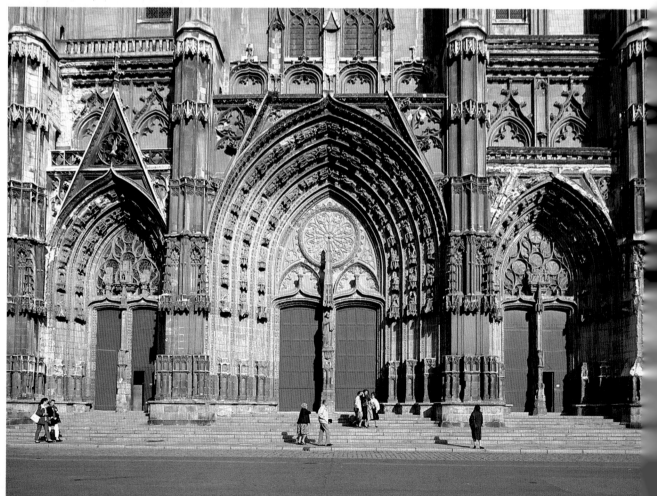

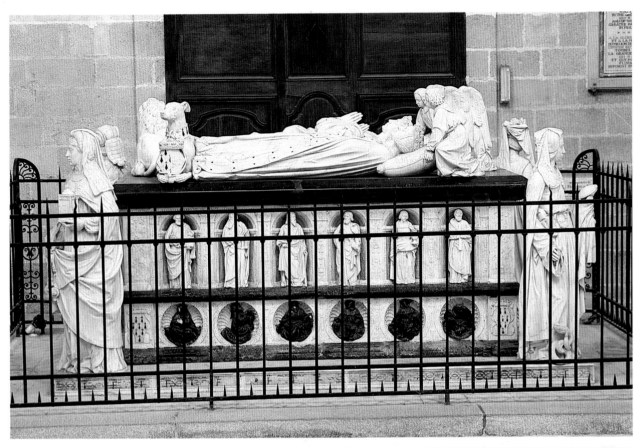

Above: the tomb of Duc François II in the cathedral. Right: panorama of the central structure.

The **castle of the dukes of Brittany** is right next to the Cathedral. Duc François II ordered its reconstruction in 1460, to replace the old 13th-century castle. Work was continued by his daughter, Anne of Brittany, whose successive marriages to King Charles VIII in 1491 and to Louis XII in 1499 were no obstacles to the ducal autonomy of which the castle was an eloquent symbol. While the massive towers and the fortified walls which overlook the moats make it a medieval fortress, the white facades of the Grand Logis indicate its scope as a residence. Large ornamental dormers and Italian style loggias testify to a Gothic art which has already breathed the air of the Renaissance. Today the castle houses a *Musée des Arts Décoratifs*, a *Musée d'Art Populaire Régional* and a *Musée d'Histoire Locale* with collections which illustrate the life and history of Nantes and of Brittany.

Alongside the castle and the cathedral, the **Cours Saint-Pierre** and **Saint-André** frame a large square decorated with a column dedicated to Louis XVI, and are flanked by gabled houses. The ensemble represents one of the

The well with seven pulleys in the inner court of the ducal castle.

Facing page: the Grand-Logis of the castle of the dukes of Brittany. Below: detail of the dormers.

The Tour des Jacobins and the moats which were dug facing the city.

loveliest urban views created in Nantes in the 18th century by the civic architects, Jean-Baptiste Ceineray and Mathurin Crucy.

But the new quarters these architects designed in the 18th century are to be found above all to the west of the medieval town, near the port. From the 16th century on, merchants from Nantes and from abroad had taken up abode on the quays. But the secondary arm of the Loire which flowed through the heart of the town before it was deviated in the 1930s no longer touches on the ancient quays where the buildings that symbolize the wealth of the 18th-century merchant city still stand. The beautiful Louix XV houses of the old **Ile Feydeau**, or the stock exchange, no longer reflect their images in the waters of the river which until recently made Nantes a small Atlantic Venice. The harmonious ensemble of facades of the **Place Royale**, behind the old quays, was created at the end of the 18th century. In 1865 the monumental fountain that forms a throne for the allegoric statues of Nantes, the

Loire and her tributaries, all by the sculptor Ducommun du Locle, was erected at its center. From here, one sees the high spire of **Saint-Nicolas**, a great neo-Gothic church designed by the architect Jean-Baptiste Lassus and begun in 1840. Further up, on the *Place Graslin*, is the Corinthian colonnade of the theater. Nearby is the **Cours Cambronne**, an elegant promenade framed by a continuous facade of houses whose charm is almost English. A statue of General Cambronne, by Debay, was set at the center in 1848.

To descend from the Quartier Graslin to the old wharves of the Loire one may take the **Passage Pommeraye**, opened in 1893. The originality of this long shopping center lies in the monumental flight of stairs which divides it in two and compensates for the slope of the terrain. The rich decor and the passers-by provide a never-ending unrehearsed spectacle.

West of the town, Thomas Dobrée, son of a Nantes industrialist, had a vast and rather odd neo-Roman Palace

built to house his sundry collections, the **Palais Dobrée**. When he died in 1895, the building became a museum which now contains an important lapidary collection, a collection of manuscripts and prints and one of objects of ancient art.

The imposing **Palais des Beaux-Arts,** built in 1893 by the architect Josso, stands near the Jardin des Plantes (Botanical Gardens). It houses a museum of painting and sculpture which can be counted among the most important in France. In addition to a collection of sculpture which illustrates the different stylistic trends of the 19th century, the collections of paintings offer a broad panorama of ancient, modern, and contemporary European art, in particular with some fine Italian primitives, a *Christ* by Solario, three masterpieces by Georges de la Tour, the *Portrait of Madame de Senones* by Ingres, the *Winnowers* by Courbet, an exceptional group of works by Kandinsky, and the *Nu Jaune* by Sonia Delaunay.

Right: facade of the Palais des Beaux-Arts, museum of painting and sculpture. Below: view of one of the museum galleries.

Facing page, above: the Passage Pommeraye and its flight of stairs. Below: the Palais Dobrée, museum of history and archaeology.

CONTENTS

ISBN 88-7009-211-9

Editor: Hubert BRISSONNEAU
Photographs from the archives of Casa Editrice Bonechi, taken by Jean-Charles PINHEIRA, with the exception of those on page 3 (Andrea Pistolesi), page 6 (Prudor) and on page 24, below (J. Carde).
Translation: Erika Pauli for Studio Comunicare, Florence.
Texts by: Jean-Jacques RIOULT (p. 4 to 20); Nicolas SIMONNET (p. 21 to 23); Philippe PETOUT (p. 24 to 37); Yves-Pascal CASTEL (p. 38 to 51); Roger BARRIÉ (p. 52 to 65/82 to 97); René LE BIHAN (p. 66 to 81); Patrick ANDRÉ (p. 98 to 119); Eric COUTUREAU (p. 120 to 127).